GREAT DINNERS
WITH LESS MEAT

Great Dinners With Less Meat

DOROTHY IVENS

With Illustrations by the Author

Prentice-Hall, Inc., Englewood Cliffs, New Jersey

Great Dinners With Less Meat by Dorothy Ivens
Copyright © 1981 by Dorothy Ivens

Printed in the United States of America
Prentice-Hall International, Inc., London
Prentice-Hall of Australia, Pty., Ltd., Sydney
Prentice-Hall of Canada, Ltd., Toronto
Prentice-Hall of India Private Ltd., New Delhi
Prentice-hall of Japan, Inc., Tokyo
Prentice-Hall of Southeast Asia Pte. Ltd., Singapore
Whitehall Books Limited, Wellington, New Zealand
10   9   8   7   6   5   4   3   2   1

Library of Congress Cataloging in Publication Data

Ivens, Dorothy.
    Great dinners with less meat.

    Includes index.
    1. Cookery (Meat)   2. Cookery (Entrées)   I. Title
TX749.I92   641.6'6   81-5058
ISBN 0-13-363788-3   AACR2
ISBN 0-13-363770-0 (pbk.)

To Penny,
with love . . .

ACKNOWLEDGMENTS

I would like to thank a few people for their help along the way—good cooks and good friends all, related or not: Penny Miller; Kate Tremper, my daughter and Santa Fe connection; Ed Romero; Mary Gandall; Philip Hall; Dale Whitt; Holly Massee; Robin Massee, who is responsible for this book's being undertaken in the first place; and last but far from least, my resident gastronome and wine expert, Bill Massee.

Dorothy Ivens

CONTENTS

Sausages and Ham

Chicken and Turkey

2. THE GLAMOUR TREATMENT—PASTRY

Phyllo Pastry

Meatballs and Sauces

... And Other Good Things With Ground Meat

6. PASTA . . . IT ISN'T ALL SPAGHETTI

7. STUFFED VEGETABLES . . . BETTER THAN YOU THINK

8. MAIN-COURSE SOUPS AND SALADS . . . FOR A CHANGE OF PACE

Main-Course Soups

Main-Course Salads

9. TOP-OF-THE-STOVE CONCOCTIONS

GREAT DINNERS
WITH LESS MEAT

ABOUT THIS BOOK

Meat is the most expensive item in the overall food budget, and the hardest to cut down. To use less meat and still provide satisfying fare is the challenge this book takes on.

The smaller amount of meat needs to be well seasoned, and the nonmeat ingredients with which it is extended should have a variety of textures and complementary flavors of their own. There are seventy such dishes here, of many different kinds, that use only one pound of meat or poultry for various numbers of servings, up to ten. A repertoire of this size makes it possible to serve interesting meals often enough for family and friends to make a noticeable dent in the food budget.

With the main course established, the question is always what to have with it. This is particularly difficult if the dish is new to you. With each main-course recipe that follows, there are suggestions and sometimes recipes for good things to round out the meal. These are given not to tie you down to a specific menu, but to give you a feeling of the sort of dish you are making. You need to know whether the accompanying vegetables should be moist or dry, firm or soft, starchy or not; whether salad should be leafy or crisp, or whether it is needed at all; how substantial a first course or dessert should be—what, in fact, would be most appropriate in taste and texture to enhance the main course. With this information implicit in the suggestions given, you can feel free to vary them according to season, availability, and your own taste.

When wines are suggested, the choices given are the ones we like with the meal. These too are not meant to limit you, but, by their nature, help to give you a sense of the food.

Incidentally, serving even the most informal meal in courses is one of the ways to help make a small amount of meat or poultry go a long way. A first course does not have to be fancy or expensive. It can be as simple as crisp vegetables or a bowl of nuts, but served with drinks or wine for the adults and soft drinks for the children. Salad can be served before the main course in the California way, or after, in the French way. Cheese—if not served before, and if the main dish is not one with cheese in it—can be served between salad and dessert. Then, with good bread, and one or more vegetables to accompany the main dish, nobody is likely to feel deprived because it has all been done with only one pound of meat.

The cooking techniques used for these recipes are varied, although a great many seem to start with the classic cooking of onions in butter or oil "until soft but not brown." Experienced cooks will find the techniques familiar, and novice cooks should not have any trouble following the carefully spelled-out directions. Some operations that sound a little difficult in words, turn out to be easy once you are doing them.

INTRODUCTION

The rule of thumb is to allow one and a half to two pounds of meat for four servings when one is buying roasts, chops, or steaks. These are the favorite cuts, easiest to cook, and the most satisfying for meat lovers. But as prices soar, it becomes impossible for most families to have that much meat very often, so we look for ways to get along on less. We watch the sales; do imaginative things with eggs, cheese, and vegetables for meatless meals; and see what can be done with a small amount of meat, stretched to go further in many different ways. If just a pound of meat can be used in recipes that yield four, six, eight, or ten servings of something satisfying and really good to eat, we can feel a little ahead of the game.

Nothing will ever take the place of a fine roast or a juicy steak. But variety is nice too, and there is plenty of inspiration in the cuisine of other countries, where using meat—with all its texture and flavor—in combination with rice, beans, grains, and pasta, has long been the way of life.

Only in the U.S. has meat, especially beef, become the main item in the country's daily diet. The production of meat is one of the nation's biggest industries, up there with cars and steel. This is likely to change as the price of meat becomes prohibitive, and as more people become aware of the terrible cost in agricultural resources for meat production.

A cow, for instance, is fed twenty-one pounds of protein to produce one pound of protein for human consumption.* Most of that twenty-one pounds of protein fed to the cow is derived from grains which could be used directly by people. Also, the vast acreage devoted to growing these grains could be used for crops that yield even more protein per acre, such as beans, peas, lentils, for example; or for leafy vegetables.

Those who worry about the contamination of meat by hormones fed to the animals, and pesticides used on the grain they eat, may—if they do not give up meat altogether—take some comfort in combining a little meat (in which the pesticide residue is high) with grains, legumes, root vegetables, etc. (in which the residue is low).

As for the nutritional aspect of cutting down on meat, only the meat industry would have us consume more rather than less, stressing the high quality of the protein in meat. Nutritionists would like us to look to other sources for some of our protein, now that heart disease, high blood pressure, even some cancers have been connected with excessive meat consumption.

Pilafs, risottos, and khoreshes are some of the classic dishes that use relatively little meat and extend it with something starchy (rice, beans, or grain). Although these extenders are high in calories, they have protein too, and other essential nutrients as well. The trick is to accompany the main dish with other foods that round out the nutrients, and avoid the calories in rich desserts. Very often just a salad is enough. Sometimes another starchy vegetable accompanies the dish because it is traditional, and in the light of modern nutritional research, turns out to complement the other starch. Rice and beans, for instance, a famous combination, supply considerably more protein when eaten at the same meal than the sum of their protein when they are eaten separately.

This book is not *primarily* concerned with nutrition. Those who are very serious about it can adapt a lot of the recipes by reading "brown rice" whenever rice is mentioned; "protein-enriched" before noodles or spaghetti; "one hundred percent whole wheat" before crusty bread. Although high-fiber bread exists and may be good, its texture is unacceptable for dinner bread.

The recipes are for meat in every form: chunks, slices, strips, and ground.

*Diet for a Small Planet, by Frances Moore Lappé, a Friends of the Earth/Ballantine Book, New York, 1971.

Sometimes a small amount of meat goes further just because of the way it is served—in crêpes, for instance, or stuffed into pasta. Pastry not only makes the meat go further, it glamorizes too.

The Chinese are masters at doing fabulous things with a tiny amount of meat. Some of the recipes borrow tricks from that cuisine.

Ground meat has all kinds of possibilities, and a great many are explored here. Since there is a lot more to making a pound of ground meat go a long way than just adding more bread crumbs, the recipes get long. More seasoning is required, for instance, and other operations are involved, needing their own lists of ingredients and accompanying methods of procedure. There is unquestionably more work than grilling a few half-pounders, but many of the dishes can be prepared ahead and cooked, heated, or assembled shortly before serving. The rewards are that you are doing something that is ecologically and nutritionally sound, you are beating the system in a small way, and creating a splendid dinner to boot.

Some of the recipes are based on traditional or other favorites, adapted for less meat; some have been developed for this book. All have been tested until I am satisfied with the taste, texture, and clarity of instructions.

Equipment

There is nothing exotic required in the way of equipment for the preparation, cooking, and serving of these dishes. Certain sizes are specified only to make sure there is enough room to accommodate the food, but not so much that it will look lost or skimpy.

A food processor is handy but not necessary except in the pasta recipe, where the hand method is not given as an alternative.

A blender, I assume, is now a standard item in most kitchens.

A food scale is not yet standard, but should be. It is a good thing to have for these recipes, all designed for one pound of meat, to weigh leftovers of cooked meat or portions of larger cuts, saving the rest for other occasions.

A meat grinder is a good thing to have . . . either an old-fashioned, hand-operated one, or one that operates on an electric mixer. Meat can be ground in a food processor, but care must be taken to not over-process. Ground meats other than beef are often hard to find, and are apt to be excessively fatty. When trimming meat to be ground, leave a little fat to supply juiciness. Most butchers will help you to estimate how much extra weight to allow for fat and bone.

A pasta machine, hand-operated, is only essential if you want to make your own pasta; and once you have tried homemade pasta, you may find the machine well worth the investment.

A large skillet, 11 to 12 inches in diameter, with a lid, is needed. Sauté pans are good too—10 to 12 inches, with lids. The skillet can be cast iron or enameled ironware. Sauté pans are usually lined copper or heavy aluminum.

A Dutch oven and flameproof ovenware casseroles, all with lids, are needed. The casseroles should be wide and shallow—2½-, 3-, 3½-, and 4-quart sizes.

Baking or au gratin dishes are needed. They come in a variety of shapes and sizes, usually 2 to 2½ inches deep. I have used rectangular ones—roughly 8 by 11, 9 by 12, and 10 by 14 inches, 2-quart, 2½-quart and 3-quart, respectively. Capacity is the best measure, and it is determined by filling the dish to the brim with water and measuring the water. I have never figured out how to do this in a store, when the dish is not marked and the salesperson doesn't know.

A large wok is nice to have if you get into the American way of using it for cooking a little meat and a lot of vegetables with or without Chinese ingredients. Real Chinese cooking is not explored in this book.

The rest of the equipment is likely to be in your kitchen already: edged cookie sheets or jelly-roll pans; 9- to 10-inch pie pans and 1-quart, straight-sided round baking dishes for deep-dish pies; and loaf pans—8-cup, 9 by 5 by 3 inches, and 5-cup, 8½ by 4½ by 2½ inches.

Ingredients

All the meat used in testing these recipes has been bought at local super-markets or the delicatessen. So has almost everything else. Fresh dill, mint, and basil were, of course, not always available, but if there was any to be had at all, the small fruit stores had it. Black beans in cans were not in every market, but a nearby one has a Spanish-Mexican-Puerto Rican section, and I found them there, as well as the canned green chilies. Ingredients for the one dish using Chinese seasonings were found in a Korean fruit market, phyllo pastry in a Greek bakery. In other words, there shouldn't be a problem with ingredients—you don't even need "a little butcher."

1. Stretch It With Rice, Beans, Grain, Vegetables, Etc., ...and Style

BEEF, VEAL, LAMB, AND PORK

Middle Eastern Beef and Kasha   6 servings

Fresh dill is essential for this tasty brown concoction, with its topping of sour cream, cucumbers, and dill.

A first course could be raw mushrooms and parsley in a lemon-and-oil dressing (recipe given), and zucchini the accompanying vegetable. A salad of thinly sliced tomatoes, green peppers, and red onion could follow or go with the dish. A big fruit salad, or melon with Porto in its hollow, along with some lacy cookies, would be a cool, refreshing finish.

A Côtes-du-Rhône or light Italian wine like Valpolicella would be good to drink with the meal.

3–3½-quart flameproof ovenware casserole, with a lid

Beef

1 pound stewing beef, in ¾-inch to 1-inch pieces	½ teaspoon salt, or to taste
2 tablespoons olive oil	¼ teaspoon freshly ground pepper
2 medium onions, coarsely chopped	2 tablespoons chopped fresh dill
2 garlic cloves, minced	2 tablespoons chopped fresh mint, or 2 teaspoons crumbled dried mint
3 tablespoons flour	½ teaspoon oregano
1 can (13¾ ounces) beef broth	1–2 teaspoons meat coloring (see **Note**)
¼ cup dry red wine	

Pat the meat dry on paper towel; it steams rather than browns if it is wet. Heat oil in a wide, heavy flameproof, lidded casserole, and brown meat on all sides. Add onions and garlic. Stir and cook until onions are transparent. Stir in flour until no white shows. Pour in broth and wine, stirring to clear bottom of pot. Stir in seasonings and meat coloring. Bring to a simmer, cover, and simmer 50–60 minutes, or until beef is tender. Check seasoning and skim off fat.

Note: For a richer brown color, you can make your own brown coloring, which doesn't affect the taste of the stew. Cook ½ cup sugar with ¼ cup water, without stirring, until it turns a rich dark brown. Holding a pot lid as a shield to protect yourself from splatter, add ¼ cup boiling water. If it is too gummy, add a little more boiling water. Stir, cool, and keep in a covered jar—it keeps indefinitely, unrefrigerated.

Kasha

1¼ cups whole kasha (buckwheat groats)	2½ cups boiling water
1 egg, beaten	1¼ teaspoons salt
2 tablespoons butter	¼ teaspoon freshly ground black pepper
2 tablespoons minced onion	

Mix kasha with egg in a lidded saucepan. Cook over low heat, stirring constantly and scraping bottom of pan. When grains separate, they need less stirring. Cook 10 minutes, 20 if you can, until grains are deep brown. Stir in butter and onion and cook until onion is transparent. Stir in water, salt, and pepper. Cover and cook on low heat 15–20 minutes, until liquid is absorbed. Fluff with a fork.

Spread meat evenly in casserole and spoon kasha over it. If either or both have cooled, do not mix them together for reheating or the kasha will soak up juices. Heat the stew, and then fluff kasha and spoon over stew. Cover and cook until kasha too is hot.

Topping

¾–1 cup sour cream at room
temperature

½ cup diced cucumber, peeled,
seeded, in ¼-inch pieces

2 tablespoons chopped fresh dill

Just before serving, spread sour cream and cucumbers, mixed together, over the kasha, and sprinkle with dill.

Raw Mushroom and Parsley Salad

¾ pound button mushrooms or
larger ones, coarsely chopped

½ cup finely chopped fresh parsley

Dressing

¼ teaspoon salt
¼ teaspoon dry mustard
⅛ teaspoon freshly ground black
pepper

2–3 tablespoons lemon juice
5 tablespoons olive oil, salad oil,
or a combination

Mix the seasonings with the lemon juice; beat in the oil. Toss the mushrooms and parsley with the dressing about an hour before serving.

Haché   *6 servings*

A pleasant spiciness characterizes this Dutch beef stew, made to go further than its pound of meat would seem to warrant, by having its accompanying potatoes warmed in its juices. Red cabbage is a traditional vegetable to have with the haché, and two recipes follow. Dark bread goes with the stew, and also with the Dutch preface to the meal—slices of Edam and Gouda cheese, followed by green pea soup, with or without dollops of sour cream and a sprinkle of chives on top.

Salad could be thinly sliced cucumbers in an oil-and-vinegar dressing; and for dessert, lemon sherbet with gingersnaps, or a bowl of fresh fruit.

Drinks can be fun with this meal, making it more of an occasion: iced Genever gin served in tiny glasses and drunk neat, with the cheese; beer with the main course; and chilled kirsch to finish.

3–4 quart Dutch oven or enameled iron casserole

1 pound round steak in 1-inch cubes	1 tablespoon Worcestershire sauce
2 tablespoons oil	2 cups beef broth
4 medium onions, chopped	6-8 medium potatoes, boiled, peeled, and halved, or 12–16 small new potatoes, boiled and peeled
3 tablespoons flour	
2 tablespoons vinegar	
2 bay leaves	
5 cloves, broken up	salt and pepper
½ teaspoon salt	¼ cup chopped parsley

Dry meat on paper towel. Heat oil in the Dutch oven or casserole, and brown meat on all sides. Add onions and cook, stirring, until they are limp and transparent. Sprinkle in the flour and stir until no white shows. Add vinegar, bay leaves, cloves, salt, Worcestershire, and broth. Bring to a simmer, cover, and cook on low heat for 1–1½ hours, or until beef is tender. Check seasonings, adding more salt if needed. Tip pot and skim off fat.

Put potatoes on top of the stew, salt and pepper them, and stir carefully into stew. Cover and cook over low heat for about 15 minutes, or until potatoes are heated. Serve sprinkled with parsley.

Red Cabbage and Apple

This is a long-cooking but flavorful version of red cabbage. It takes about an hour to cook, so it can be done at the same time as the stew. For a crisper but less succulent version, which takes less time, see the recipe following this one.

1 medium red cabbage, shredded
  (6–8 cups)
2 tablespoons butter
2 medium onions, chopped
2 tart apples, peeled, cored, and
  sliced
2 tablespoons brown sugar

¼ cup red wine
¼ cup water
½ teaspoon salt
¼ teaspoon black pepper
⅛ teaspoon ground cloves
⅛ teaspoon cayenne pepper

Trim any bad outer leaves from cabbage, quarter and core it. Cut across in ½-inch slices. In a 2½- or 3-quart lidded flameproof casserole, melt the butter. Slowly cook the onions and apples in the butter until the onions are limp and transparent. Add the sugar and continue cooking until the apples are soft and glazed. Add wine, water, seasonings, and cabbage. Bring to a simmer, cover and cook on very low heat for 45–60 minutes.

Quick-Cooking Red Cabbage

1 medium red cabbage,
    6–8 cups shredded
½ teaspoon salt
¼ teaspoon pepper

½ cup water
2 tablespoons vinegar
  butter

Trim, quarter, and core cabbage. Cut across in ¼-inch slices. Place in lidded flameproof casserole with salt, pepper, water, and vinegar. Cover and cook about 5 minutes, until cabbage is just tender but still crisp. Drain, butter, and serve.

Beef and Bulgur   *6 servings*

The stew part of this combination is not expanded, but the bulgur is, with the addition of zucchini. The bulgur has a nice chewy quality because it is soaked, rather than cooked, before heating with the zucchini. Served together with crusty bread, or hot pita bread, the combination makes adequate portions for six; four people can have a feast.

To enrich and glamorize the meal, a fancy salad of avocado, carrots, and oranges (recipe given) could go along with or follow the main course, and something from a Greek pastry shop could end it.

Before the meal, one could sip Ouzo and eat pita bread with some feta cheese and watercress. For those who like it, there is the Greek wine, Retsina, to drink with the meal; others might prefer a Rioja or a Zinfandel.

Serve in 2½-quart baking dish (approximately 12 by 9 by 2 inches)

Bulgur

1½ cups bulgur
  1 teaspoon salt

3 cups boiling water

Mix the bulgur with the salt in a medium-sized bowl, and pour the boiling water into it. Allow to stand for 1 hour.

Stew

1 pound stewing beef, in ¾-inch
  to 1-inch pieces
2 tablespoons oil
2 medium onions, chopped
  (2 cups)
2 garlic cloves, minced
½ teaspoon salt
¼ teaspoon freshly ground black
  pepper

1 tablespoon chopped fresh mint,
  or 1 teaspoon crumbled
  dried mint
1 teaspoon oregano
½ cup tomato purée
1½ cups beef broth

Pat the beef dry. Heat the oil in a large, heavy skillet, and when a light haze appears, put in the meat and brown a few pieces at a time. As the pieces are browned, put them into the 2½–3-quart heavy saucepan or flameproof casserole with lid. Add onions and garlic to the meat, and stir over low heat until onions are soft. Stir in salt, pepper, mint and oregano. Add tomato purée and broth. Bring to a boil, turn down to a simmer, cover, and simmer 1–1½ hours, or until beef is tender. Tip pot and skim off fat. Taste and add salt if needed. When stew is done, keep warm on lowest heat, or in a 200°F oven.

Zucchini

2 zucchini, 7 to 8 inches
  (about 1 pound)

3 tablespoons olive oil
  salt, pepper, oregano
  the soaked bulgur

Wash and trim ends off the zucchini. Scrape away any flawed spots, but do not peel. Cut into 4 lengthwise and make ⅜-inch cuts across. Heat the olive oil in the skillet and cook the zucchini over fairly high heat until there are a few brown spots, but zucchini is still firm. Sprinkle with salt, pepper, and oregano.

Assembly and Finish

mint and lemon juice to taste   fresh mint leaves or parsley
                                                    for garnish

Drain the bulgur, pressing in a sieve to get as much moisture out as possible.

Add the bulgur to the zucchini, and stir over lower heat to mix and to warm the bulgur. Stir in the mint, and when the mixture is thoroughly heated, add the lemon.

Lift the meat out of its sauce and place in the middle of the heated baking dish or au gratin pan. Fluff the bulgur mixture around the meat, and either pour all the sauce over the meat, or just some, saving the rest to serve in a little bowl. If you have fresh mint, scatter a few chopped or whole leaves over the stew and bulgur; otherwise garnish with parsley.

Orange, Carrot, and Avocado Salad

 3 cups coarsely grated carrots
½ cup orange juice
¼ teaspoon salt
¼ teaspoon grated fresh ginger
    root, or ⅛ teaspoon dried
    ginger
  drop or two of Tabasco, or to
    taste

1 small head Boston lettuce,
    broken up, washed, and dried
2 small navel oranges, peeled
    (leaving no white), and thinly
    sliced
1 large ripe avocado, peeled,
    seeded, and sliced
2 tablespoons lemon juice

Put carrots into a bowl and mix thoroughly with the combination of orange juice, salt, ginger, and Tabasco. Allow to stand for an hour.

Arrange lettuce around the edge of a serving dish. Make a mound of the carrots in the middle, saving the juice they have been in. Place orange slices over carrots and avocado slices on top. Sprinkle lemon juice over the carrots and avocado slices, and juice from the carrots over all.

Piquant Beef With Vegetables   *6–8 servings*

This spicy concoction consists of a barbecue sauce with the meat cooked in it, and cooked potatoes added to heat in the mixture. Fresh whole green beans, cooked to the point of tender crispness, and still bright green, would be the perfect vegetable to have with it. Salad, crusty bread, cheese, and fruit could round out the repast. To make the meal more formal or more filling, serve a first course—soup, artichokes vinaigrette, or hard-boiled eggs on lettuce, with mayonnaise, to name a few possibilities.

Beer is good with this meal, or a sturdy red wine that will stand up to the spiciness, like a Premiat from Romania, or a Chianti.

3–3½ quart casserole

1 small onion, minced	2 tablespoons oil
1 cup tomato purée	1 pound stewing beef, in ¾-inch
1 cup beef broth	to 1-inch pieces
3 tablespoons vinegar	salt and pepper
2 tablespoons Worcestershire	2 tablespoons flour
sauce	1 large green pepper, seeded,
½ teaspoon salt	in ½-inch pieces
2 teaspoons paprika	6–8 potatoes, boiled, peeled, and
2 teaspoons chili powder	halved
¼ teaspoon cinnamon	10–12 pitted black olives
⅛ teaspoon ground cloves	chopped parsley

In a heavy, lidded flameproof casserole, combine first 10 ingredients in the order listed, and bring to a boil. Lower heat and let simmer while you prepare the meat.

Heat the oil in a heavy skillet and brown the beef pieces on all sides, sprinkling with salt and pepper. Stir in the flour until no white shows, and scrape the meat into the casserole. Bring to a simmer, cover, and simmer for 1–1½ hours, or until beef is just tender. Add green pepper after ¾ hour of cooking. When meat is tender, tip pot and skim off fat. Taste to check seasoning. Add more salt if needed.

Put the cooked potatoes into the casserole, sprinkling with salt and pepper, and then stir carefully into the stew. Cover and heat, stirring occasionally, until potatoes are heated through—15–20 minutes. Serve with black olives and parsley strewn over the top.

As is the case with all stews, this may be done in the oven instead of on top of the stove. Preheat the oven to 325°F, and after combining meat and sauce, bring to a boil, cover, and place in the oven. The timing is about the same.

Veal and Rice With Gremolata *4–5 servings*

Gremolata is an Italian garnish that not only decorates the food, but adds a magic fillip to the taste. It is a mixture of freshly chopped parsley, minced garlic, and grated lemon rind.

Zucchini, lightly sautéed in olive oil, with a sprinkle of salt, pepper, and oregano, goes with the dish, along with good crusty bread. A hearty soup wouldn't be too heavy to start the meal; salad could be spinach with some sliced mushrooms, and dessert Italian cheeses—Bel Paese, Taleggio, Fontina—and fruit.

Chilled white wine from Italy—Pinot Grigio, Verdicchio, Soave, or California's Sauvignon Blanc, which is also called Blanc Fumé or Fumé Blanc, would be splendid with this fine dish.

2½–3-quart shallow, flameproof, lidded casserole

Stew

2 tablespoons oil, preferably olive oil	2 tablespoons tomato paste
	¼ cup dry white wine
1 pound stewing veal, boneless, in ¾-inch to 1-inch pieces	½ teaspoon salt
	¼ teaspoon white pepper
2 medium onions, finely chopped	½ teaspoon thyme
2 garlic cloves, minced	½ teaspoon basil
3 tablespoons flour	1 small bay leaf
1¼ cups chicken broth	1 wide strip lemon peel

Heat the oil in a casserole. Pat the veal pieces dry with paper towel and brown them lightly in the oil. Add the onions and garlic and cook on low heat, stirring, until onions are limp and transparent. Sprinkle in flour and stir until no white shows.

Mix the tomato paste with the wine and add to the casserole with the chicken broth. Stir to clear the bottom of the pan. Stir in the seasonings and lemon peel and bring to a simmer. Cover and simmer for 1–1½ hours, or until meat is tender.

Rice

1 cup uncooked rice   2 cups chicken broth

Add rice to boiling chicken broth. Stir once, cover, and lower heat. Cook for 20 minutes, or until liquid is absorbed. Fluff with a fork. Spread the stew evenly on the bottom of the casserole, and spoon the rice over it lightly.

Gremolata

⅓ cup finely chopped parsley   2 tablespoons grated lemon rind
 1 teaspoon minced garlic

Mix together the parsley, garlic, and grated lemon rind (the gremolata) and sprinkle on top.

Serve with Parmesan cheese in a small bowl for those who want it.

To prepare ahead: Stew and rice may be fully cooked ahead, but do not combine them until just before serving time, or the rice will absorb the stew juices. Gremolata may be prepared and wrapped in plastic until serving time. About 10 or 15 minutes before serving, heat the stew, fluff the rice and scatter lightly over the stew, cover, and heat just until rice is hot. Sprinkle with the gremolata and serve.

Sherried Veal and Noodles   *6 servings*

There is a kind of elegance to a veal dish, even in the form of a stew, and with noodles. It isn't just the high price of veal, because stewing veal should not be too expensive, especially when you only need a pound. In this version, it could be the slight translucence of a cornstarch-thickened sauce that does it.

In this case, to round out the meal in appropriate simple style, the first course could be Nova Scotia salmon, with cucumbers in a sour cream and dill sauce (recipe follows); the accompanying vegetable artichokes; a watercress and endive salad; a tray of two or three great cheeses; good crusty bread all the way through the meal; and a fabulous pastry for dessert.

A light red wine served cool (an hour on the bottom shelf of the refrigerator) is pleasant with the veal—a Beaujolais Villages, Bardolino, or Valpolicella, or one of the California Gamays.

Serve in a 2½-quart baking dish (9 by 12 inches, approximately)

Veal

2 slices bacon
1 tablespoon butter
1 pound stewing veal in ¾-inch to
    1-inch pieces
2 teaspoons minced fresh ginger,
    or ½ teaspoon dried ginger
2 garlic cloves, minced
¼ teaspoon ground nutmeg
½ teaspoon dried mustard
⅓ cup Amontillado (medium dry)
    Sherry

½ teaspoon salt
½ teaspoon white pepper
½ teaspoon marjoram
2 cups chicken broth, warmed
    (remove fat from the top)
2 teaspoons meat coloring (see
    Middle Eastern Beef and
    Kasha)
1 tablespoon cornstarch

Cook the bacon in a heavy pot or casserole until it is crisp and golden. Set aside on paper towel. Remove all but 1 tablespoon fat from the casserole and add the butter. When butter stops foaming, pat the meat dry on paper towel and cook in the fat until no pink shows, and there are spots of brown on the pieces. Stir in the ginger, garlic, nutmeg, mustard, and Sherry. Cook over medium-high heat until Sherry has almost evaporated. Add salt, pepper, and marjoram. Pour in the broth, and stir to clear the bottom of the pan. Bring to a simmer, cover, and simmer for 50–60 minutes or until veal is tender. Tip pot and skim off any fat. Taste and add salt if needed. Stir in cornstarch dissolved in a little cold water. Cook just until sauce thickens. It should have a creamy consistency. Add a little more cornstarch mixed with water, if needed.

Assembly and Finish

¾ pound mushrooms, lightly
    sautéed in 1–2 tablespoons
    butter
12 ounces thin noodles

3–4 ounces slivered almonds,
    toasted
the bacon, crumbled
⅓ cup chopped parsley

Mushrooms and noodles may be prepared while the stew cooks. Trim ends of mushrooms. Leave small ones whole, and cut large ones to the same size, more or less. Sauté them lightly (not long enough for juices to come out) in 1–2 tablespoons butter, and stir into the stew.

Cook noodles according to package directions, drain, and put back in their cooking pot with 1 tablespoon butter. Sprinkle with a little salt and white pepper, and mix. Pour into a warm, buttered 12-by-9-inch baking dish, and spoon stew and mushrooms over them. Serve sprinkled with almonds, crumbled bacon, and parsley.

Cucumbers in Sour Cream and Dill Sauce

1 cup sour cream
1 tablespoon chopped fresh dill
  salt to taste

¼ teaspoon white pepper
1 teaspoon lemon juice
2 medium cucumbers

Mix sauce ingredients. Peel and halve cucumbers, remove seeds, cut across in ½-inch pieces, and stir into sauce.

Lamb With White Beans and Artichokes   *6–8 servings*

Lamb, rosemary, garlic, and artichokes seem to belong together, and white beans complement them all in this hearty dish. Since the lamb is not browned before stewing, and the beans are white, the garnish of parsley is very important. Half the parsley is stirred in to add flavor and carry the color accent throughout the dish. The rest is strewn over the top.

This is not a difficult recipe, but the beans do take a long time. Some canned beans are not too bad—red kidney, black turtle, and garbanzos—but white beans seem to be too soft in cans. Dried beans, although they have to soak for an hour and can take as long as 1½ hours to cook, come out properly firm. Since the whole concoction improves with standing, you might want to make it ahead.

Broiled tomatoes would supply a nice touch of color with the lamb and beans, and salad could be full of crisp things like radishes, celery, etc. To make the meal an occasion, caramel custard could end it.

A St. Émilion from Bordeaux, not too old, is good to drink with the dish.

Serve in 3-quart casserole or 2½-quart baking dish (12 by 9 by 2 inches, approximately)

Beans

1 pound dried white beans, Great Northern or navy	8 cups water 2½ teaspoons salt

Wash and pick over 1 pound beans (slightly more than 2 cups), discarding foreign matter and shriveled beans. Cover with 8 cups water and bring to a boil. Remove from heat, cover, and allow to soak for an hour. Bring to a boil, turn down heat, and simmer, partially covered, for 30 minutes. Add 2½ teaspoons salt and simmer 15 minutes longer, or more. Timing for beans is irritatingly imprecise, so keep checking.

Beans are done when they are tender but not mushy; the skin flutters and lifts when you blow on them. Drain the beans when you are satisfied that they are done. Save the cooking liquid; it makes a fine soup base.

Lamb

2 tablespoons butter
1 pound boneless lamb shoulder,
    in ¾-inch to 1-inch pieces
2 medium onions, coarsely
    chopped
2 garlic cloves, minced
3 tablespoons flour
1 can (13¾ ounces) beef broth
¾ teaspoon rosemary leaves,
    crushed

1 bay leaf
½ teaspoon salt
⅛ teaspoon cayenne pepper
2 14-ounce cans artichoke
    hearts, drained, or
    2 packages frozen artichoke
    hearts, cooked and drained
    (see **Note**)

½ cup finely chopped parsley

In a casserole with a lid, heat the butter and put in lamb, onions, and garlic. Cook over low heat, stirring, until lamb has lost its color, and onions are limp but not brown. This takes about 15 minutes. Sprinkle in flour and stir until no white shows. Stir in broth, rosemary, bay leaf, salt, and cayenne. Cover pot and simmer for 40–60 minutes, or until lamb is tender. Tip pot and skim off fat. Check seasoning. Stew should have a good strong taste to permeate the beans that will be added.

When the beans are done, stir them carefully into the stew, and tuck in the artichoke hearts. If you are serving in the casserole, heat on the top of the stove until everything is piping hot. To serve in a baking dish, turn into a heated baking dish, cover loosely with foil, and heat in a preheated 350°F oven for about 30 minutes. Gently stir in half the parsley, and sprinkle the rest on top.

To prepare ahead: Cook either the stew or the beans, or both, as above. Cover loosely with foil until they cool, then cover tightly and refrigerate. If both stew and beans are done ahead, complete the dish in the vessel it is to be served in, omitting the parsley. Bring to room temperature, then heat, loosely covered with foil, in a preheated 350°F oven for about 30 minutes. Finish as above.

Note: Canned artichokes, although a bit soft, have a pleasant lemony taste. Frozen ones can be cooked to a firmer texture, and improved with a squeeze of lemon.

Lamb Pilaf   *5–6 servings*

Pilaf or pilau is an Eastern rice dish containing all sorts of good things—nuts, fruit, meat—alone or together. In this one we have prunes, raisins, and lamb in the rice, which is moderately hot in taste and golden with curry. It is not as sweet as you might expect. And there's the fun of sprinkling the pilaf with condiments from little side dishes: toasted slivered almonds, minced orange or lemon peel, tiny gherkins, shredded coconut, chopped hard-boiled eggs, as well as the usual chutney. Spinach with a touch of nutmeg would go well with the pilaf; a green salad with lots of cucumbers could follow. For dessert, a big bowl of nuts in their shells and ripe mangoes, or a lime or lemon sherbert served with macaroons.

Wine doesn't go well with curry; beer or iced tea would be better.

2½–3-quart lidded flameproof casserole, preferably wide and shallow

Stew

1 slice bacon, diced	⅛ teaspoon crushed red pepper
1 tablespoon oil	1 teaspoon turmeric
1 pound stewing lamb, in ¾-inch to 1-inch pieces	1 teaspoon curry powder
	1 cup canned beef broth
1 medium onion, chopped (about 1 cup)	1 small bay leaf
	6 thin lemon slices
½ teaspoon salt	
¼ teaspoon freshly ground black pepper	

In a casserole with a lid, slowly cook the bacon in the oil until it is golden. Push to the side of the casserole. Add the lamb pieces, a few at a time. Cook and stir the lamb until no red shows and there are spots of brown. Push to the side with the bacon. When all the lamb is done, pour off the fat in the casserole.

Add the onion, stir and cook on low heat until onion is limp. Stir in salt, pepper, red pepper, turmeric, and curry. Pour in the broth, add bay leaf and lemon. Bring to a boil, turn down to a simmer, cover, and simmer for 30 minutes.

Rice and Fruit Additions

10–12 pitted prunes, quartered

½ cup yellow seedless raisins

1⅔ cups canned beef broth

1¼ cups rice

lemon slices

¼ cup chopped parsley

Add the prunes, raisins, and broth. Bring to a boil, add rice, stir once, and turn down to a simmer. Cover and simmer 30–40 minutes longer, or until meat is tender and rice has swollen and absorbed liquid. The dish should be moist but not wet. Add a little broth or water if it is too dry.

Pick out the remnants of lemon slices, and the bay leaf, if you can find them. Squeeze in some lemon, arrange fresh lemon slices down the middle, and sprinkle parsley over the whole thing.

Szekely Goulash   *6–8 servings*

Sauerkraut and pork are the main ingredients in this Transylvanian goulash. Before the pork goes in, the sauerkraut cooks for an hour, which seems excessive, but it does wonderful things for the taste. Sour cream is stirred in at the end, and boiled potatoes, a classic accompaniment, are put in to heat and pick up flavor from the goulash.

A basket of assorted breads—pumpernickel, rye, and Italian—could accompany the goulash, and could also go with some Gouda or Edam cheese before it. A leafy salad, including some spinach, and a fruity dessert is all you need to round out a splendid meal.

The adventurous might like to try the white wines of Austria with this— like Gumpoldskirchener or those of Krems. Young, fruity red wine goes with it too, also beer.

3–4-quart lidded flameproof casserole

Sauerkraut

2 slices bacon, diced	6–8 juniper berries, and/or
2 medium onions, chopped	2 tablespoons gin
2 garlic cloves, minced	2 cups dry white wine
2 pounds sauerkraut	canned chicken broth, if
1 teaspoon caraway seeds	needed, to barely cover
12 whole peppercorns, bruised	sauerkraut

In a casserole, slowly cook the bacon until it has rendered its fat and is golden brown. Add the onions and garlic; cook slowly until they are soft but not brown. Drain sauerkraut and squeeze out juice with the hands. Mix thoroughly with onions, garlic, and bacon. Stir in caraway seeds, peppercorns, juniper berries or gin (or both), and wine. Add some chicken broth if wine does not quite cover the sauerkraut. Cover and cook on top of the stove, or in a preheated 325°F oven, for 1 hour. Check occasionally, adding more broth if sauerkraut dries.

Pork

2 tablespoons oil

1 pound stewing pork in 1-inch pieces

½ teaspoon salt

2 tablespoons Hungarian paprika

1 can (1 pound) Italian tomatoes, drained and chopped (reserve liquid in case stew needs moistening later; if not, save for other uses)

Heat the oil in a large heavy skillet. Dry the pork on paper towels, and brown the pieces on all sides. Drain them when they are done on paper towels. Pour fat from the skillet, return pork, sprinkle with salt and paprika, and mix well. Stir tomatoes into skillet with the pork, and add the mixture to the sauerkraut in the casserole. Cover and continue cooking on the stove top or in the oven for 1–1½ hours, or until pork is tender. Check during cooking to see if moisture is needed—mixture should be thick but not dry. Add tomato liquid or more broth if needed. Tip pot and skim off any fat, and check seasoning, adding more salt if necessary.

Assembly and Finish

6–8 medium potatoes, boiled, peeled and halved

½–1 cup sour cream

2 teaspoons grated lemon rind

2 pimientos, chopped

Carefully stir in the potatoes, cover, and heat for about 15 minutes until potatoes are heated. Stir in sour cream, and heat to warm through but not to boil. Serve sprinkled with lemon rind and pimientos.

Pork, Pears, Pecans, and Brown Rice   *6–8 servings*

Pork and pears together in a stew is a German idea. In working out the rest of the ingredients to enhance that combination, pecans just happened to fit in; they were not added only for the sake of alliteration.

For those who like the nutrition value—and taste—of rice and beans in the same meal, a salad of black beans vinaigrette is recommended. To carry through on a German theme for a hot vegetable, it could be green cabbage, cooked until tender-crisp and still green, with a sprinkle of caraway seeds; for bread, black or rye; for dessert, strudel, or stewed fruit and gingerbread.

For wine, try a Riesling or Sylvaner from the Rhine or California.

4-quart casserole with lid

Rice

2 cups brown rice

5 cups water

1½ teaspoons salt

1 tablespoon butter

Put rice into boiling water with salt and butter. Bring to a boil again, stir once, and turn down heat. Cover and cook on low heat for 45–55 minutes, until liquid has evaporated. Fluff with fork and keep warm.

Pork

1 pound boneless stewing pork in ¾-inch pieces

2 tablespoons oil, more if needed

2 medium onions, coarsely chopped

2 garlic cloves, minced

⅓ cup dry white wine or dry Vermouth

1¾ cups chicken broth

1 teaspoon salt

¼ teaspoon salt

¼ teaspoon white pepper

2 teaspoons minced fresh ginger, or ½ teaspoon dried ground ginger

½ teaspoon rosemary leaves, crumbled

¼ teaspoon allspice

2 pounds firm pears (choose pears *slightly* soft around the stem)

juice of 1 lemon

Pat the meat dry with paper towel. Heat the oil in a large, heavy skillet until a haze appears. Put in the meat, a few pieces at a time, and cook until no red shows and there are spots of brown here and there. As the pieces are done, put them into a heavy, lidded 4-quart saucepan or casserole. Add the onions and garlic to the meat, and cook over medium heat until onions are beginning to be transparent. Pour in the wine, turn up the heat, and cook until wine has almost evaporated. Add the broth, stirring to clear the bottom of the pan. Stir in salt, pepper, ginger, rosemary, and allspice. Cover and simmer for 25 minutes.

Peel and core pears, and cut into ¾-inch cubes. As you prepare the pears, squeeze lemon over them to keep them white. Add pears to the stew, with the lemon juice. Cover saucepan or casserole and cook another 15 minutes, or until pork is tender. Don't worry about the pears, they are good firm or soft.

Assembly and Finish

2 ounces (¾ cup) whole pecans,   chopped parsley
    lightly sautéed in
    1 teaspoon butter

To serve, fluff rice over the stew. Lightly sauté the pecans in butter and scatter over rice. Sprinkle parsley on top.

SAUSAGES AND HAM

Sausages and Vegetables

6 servings

Potatoes do the main extending in this dish; onions, green peppers, zucchini, and tomatoes do the rest. Although a pound of Italian sausages is not a great deal for six people, it is enough to send the wonderful flavor through the vegetables, and there are plenty of them. Hot sausage is used here for its strong taste, but the sweet ones are good too. If sweet sausages are used, add a few pinches of crushed fennel seeds for extra flavor without the hotness.

Serve with a big green salad and crusty bread. Some Italian cheeses—Taleggio, Bel Paese, and Gorgonzola, for instance—and fruit could round out the meal. Chianti Classico or Rioja are good wines to go with both the sausage dish and the cheeses.

4-quart flameproof, lidded casserole

1 pound Italian hot sausage
1 tablespoon oil
2 medium onions, coarsely
    chopped
2 medium green peppers,
    in ½-inch strips
2 medium zucchini,
    in ¾-inch slices
3 garlic cloves, minced
    salt

    pepper (optional)
2 teaspoons dried oregano
2 cans (1 pound each) Italian
    tomatoes, coarsely chopped
¾ cup grated Parmesan or
    Romano cheese
6 medium potatoes, peeled,
    in ⅛-inch slices

Prick the sausages and put them into a casserole with the oil. Cook over low heat until the sausages are well browned, turning often. Set aside to drain on paper towel.

Pour off all but 2 tablespoons of the accumulated fat from the casserole and put in the onions. Cook, stirring until they begin to get limp. Stir in the green peppers, zucchini, and garlic, sprinkling with salt, pepper if used, and 1 teaspoon of the oregano. Cook for about 5 minutes, stirring gently.

Mix in the tomatoes, sprinkling with salt, optional pepper, the rest of the oregano, and the cheese. Stir to incorporate any morsels stuck to the bottom. Add the sausages, cut into ½-inch slices. Check seasoning.

Remove one half of this mixture (to a large bowl), and cover what is left in the casserole with the potatoes, sprinkling with salt and optional pepper. Return the other half of the vegetable mixture to cover the potatoes.

Cover the casserole and place in a preheated 350°F oven for 30–45 minutes, or until potatoes are cooked and zucchini is tender but not soft.

Sausages and Black Beans   *6 servings*

Hot Italian sausages are used here because their good strong taste flavors a lot of beans. For those wary of hotness, though, sweet Italian or "break-fast" sausages may be used, cooked and sliced as indicated in this recipe. There is no salt called for in the list of ingredients because the canned beans used were well salted, but brands differ, so check and add salt if needed.

This dish improves with standing.

First course could be South American or Spanish appetizers (tapas), and a list of suggestions for them is given. For the main course, top each serving with a slice or two of orange, and serve with rice, a sliced tomato salad, and sprigs of parsley or watercress for a stunning color scheme.

Since this is a somewhat Brazilian dish, and they like bananas and coconut, dessert could be sliced bananas with sour cream sweetened with brown sugar, and shredded coconut on top; or something fabulous like bananas sliced lengthwise, sautéed in butter, flamed in Triple Sec, and sprinkled with coconut and slivered almonds.

Red jug wines, from Spain or Italy, are fine with this.

2½-quart flameproof casserole

1 pound hot Italian sausage	2 bay leaves
1 tablespoon oil	4 teaspoons vinegar
2 medium onions, coarsely chopped	4 teaspoons cornstarch pinch of crushed red chili
2 cloves garlic, minced	peppers (optional)
3 cans (1 pound each) black beans, 1 can drained, liquid reserved	2 navel oranges, peeled and thinly sliced in rounds

Prick the sausages and put them into a heavy flameproof casserole, with the oil. Cook over medium heat until they are well browned, turning often. Set them aside on paper towels. Pour off all but about 2 tablespoons of the accumulated fat from the skillet, and put in the onions and garlic. Cook over low heat, stirring, until the onions are limp and transparent but not browned.

Add the beans, bay leaves, vinegar mixed with the cornstarch, and hot pepper, if used. Add the sausages, cut into 1-inch pieces. Cook uncovered over low heat, stirring often, for 15 minutes, or until heated through. Use the reserved bean liquid if needed for extra moisture. Add salt if needed. Serve topped with orange slices.

For later serving: cool, loosely covered, to room temperature and refrigerate. Reheat on top of the stove, stirring frequently, or place in preheated 350°F oven, covered, for 20 to 30 minutes.

Suggestions for Appetizers, Spanish Style *(Tapas)*

Pimientos or roasted red peppers, whole, with olive oil and minced garlic
Black olives with olive oil, a little vinegar, minced onions, and oregano
Pickled beets with onion rings
Canned green chilies
Tiny canned shrimp in olive oil with red-pepper flakes and chopped parsley
Raw mushrooms with oil, lemon, salt, pepper, and parsley
Potato salad with garlic in it
Salted almonds
Roasted peanuts

Polenta and Sausages   *8 servings*

Polenta is cornmeal, and it can be found in bulk in some Italian food stores. American packaged cornmeal is easier to find and does very well as a substitute. The hot, cooked cornmeal is spread in a baking dish and the sauce with sausages poured over. Hot Italian sausages are used in this recipe because the cornmeal seems to need their strong flavor. However, if the taste of sweet Italian sausage is preferred, they may be used, with a little dish of hot red-pepper flakes served on the side to be added at each person's discretion. Artichokes or green beans could be served with the polenta, either hot, or cold with a vinaigrette sauce. If the vegetable is served hot, salad could be thinly sliced zucchini and radishes, with scallions, in an oil-and-lemon dressing.

Antipasto could start the meal (suggestions given), and lime or lemon sherbet with a dollop or two of Cointreau could finish it off.

A Rioja, Chianti Classico, or Romanian Premiat would be a good wine for both first and main courses.

2½-quart baking dish (12 by 9 by 2 inches, approximately)

Polenta

2 cups cornmeal

2 quarts water

2 teaspoons salt

2 tablespoons butter

Sprinkle cornmeal into rapidly boiling salted water, stirring constantly to prevent lumps from forming. Turn down heat and cook, stirring often, for 30–35 minutes. Stir in butter and spread in baking dish. Keep warm until sauce is cooked.

Sauce

1 pound Italian hot sausage

1 tablespoon olive oil

2 medium onions, finely chopped

2 garlic cloves, minced

1 cup beef broth

2 tablespoons tomato paste

1 can (1 pound, 13 ounces)
    Italian tomatoes, chopped
    or mashed

1 teaspoon dried basil, or
    1 tablespoon chopped fresh
    basil

1 teaspoon oregano

1 bay leaf
    salt and pepper

1 large green pepper, seeded,
    deribbed, coarsely chopped

½ cup Parmesan cheese

Prick the sausages and put them into a wide, heavy skillet with the oil. Cook on low heat for 10–12 minutes until they are browned. Set aside on paper towel. Pour off all but a film of oil from the skillet, and in it cook the onions and garlic until the onions are limp. Add broth and stir in tomato paste, clearing bottom of pan. Bring to a boil, then simmer for 5 minutes. Add tomatoes, basil, oregano, bay leaf, and salt and pepper to taste. Don't make it too bland. Simmer for 30 minutes. Add sausages, each cut into 4 pieces, and green pepper. Cook 10 minutes longer, until green pepper is lightly cooked but still firm.

Pour sauce over the polenta and sprinkle with Parmesan cheese. Place in 350°F oven for 15 minutes, or until piping hot.

Suggestions for Antipasto

Sardines
Green and black olives
Pimientos
Green and red sweet-pepper strips
Celery and cucumber strips
Scallions with green tops
Hot chili peppers
Fennel in thin strips
Hard-boiled egg halves with capers
Provolone cheese
Radishes
Tomatoes in wedges
Watercress

Polenta and Ham   8 servings

Easy and substantial, this polenta dish, like the preceding one with sausages, makes good family or party fare. To make it into party fare, all it needs is a first course of shrimp, clams on the half shell, or steamed mussels. Salad could be Boston lettuce with blanched cauliflower and shallots. Dessert could be something chocolate—ice cream, cake, or a mousse.

To drink with the meal, try a Muscadet or Pinot Grigio.

2½-quart baking dish (12 by 9 by 2 inches, approximately)

cooked polenta (see Polenta
   and Sausages)
1 pound cooked ham, sliced
¼ pound Jarlsberg, Swiss, or
   Gruyère cheese, coarsely
   grated
1 tablespoon oil
1 medium onion, finely
   chopped
1 garlic clove, minced

1 can (1 pound, 13 ounces)
   Italian tomatoes, chopped or
   mashed
1 teaspoon oregano
   salt and pepper
¾ cup fine dry bread crumbs
½ cup grated Parmesan cheese

¼ cup finely chopped parsley

Pour the cooked polenta into the baking dish and smooth the top. Cut the ham slices in half and lay them over the polenta in 2 long rows. Sprinkle the cheese on top. Cover lightly while you make the sauce.

In a saucepan, heat the oil and cook the onion and garlic for a minute or two, until onion is limp. Add the tomatoes, oregano, and salt and pepper to taste. Cook for 15 minutes, then pour over the cheese layer.

Mix together the bread crumbs and Parmesan, and sprinkle over the tomato layer. Place in preheated 350°F oven for 20–25 minutes, or until hot, bubbling, and a little brown on top. Serve sprinkled with parsley.

Puff-Topped Ham, Rice, and Broccoli   8 servings

The cream-puff topping (not sweet, by the way) on creamy layers of rice, broccoli, and ham not only makes this dish handsome to behold, but it helps to make 8 ample servings using only a pound of ham. The puff-shell dough is surprisingly easy to make, although it takes a little muscle if made by hand. Made in a food processor, it couldn't be easier. Both methods are given here.

A fresh, cool starter for the meal could be seviche, scallops "cooked" by standing in lime and lemon juices and seasonings for a few hours (recipe given). Spinach would be a good accompanying vegetable. A relish that adds a sharp, fruity accent is one made with apricots and horseradish (recipe given). A leafy green salad, then a sherbet, could follow.

White wine goes with the whole meal—a Muscadet or a not-too-sweet German wine such as a Moselle Kabinett.

3-quart baking dish (14 by 10 by 2 inches, approximately)

1½ cups rice
  3 cups chicken broth
  1 bunch broccoli
  4 tablespoons butter (½ stick)
  ¼ cup finely chopped shallots, or
     ½ cup chopped scallions,
      white part only
  ½ teaspoon thyme
  3 tablespoons flour

3 cups milk
1 tablespoon Dijon mustard
2 tablespoons Cream Sherry
1 pound cooked ham,
    in ¼-inch dice
    salt and pepper
8–10 ounces sharp cheddar
    cheese, in thin slices

Bring the broth to a boil in a 2–3-quart lidded saucepan. Stir in the rice, cover, lower heat to simmer, and cook 20 minutes. Spread in a buttered baking dish.

Wash broccoli and cut flowerets into uniform sizes, including small stems. Peel large stems down to the tender pale green, and slice diagonally in ¼-inch slices. Cook in a large pot of boiling salted water for 5 minutes, or until broccoli is bright green and just barely tender. Drain at once, and spread over the rice.

Melt butter in a saucepan, add shallots or scallions and thyme. Cook a minute or two, stirring, until shallots or scallions are soft. Remove from the heat and stir in flour to make a smooth paste. Add milk, stir to blend well, and put back on the heat. Cook, stirring, until sauce thickens. Add mustard, Sherry, ham, and salt and pepper to taste. When sauce is cool, pour it over the broccoli, and lay cheese slices on top to cover.

Puff-Shell Topping

⅔ cup water

4 tablespoons butter (½ stick)

½ teaspoon salt

1 cup flour

4 large eggs

Make the topping when you are ready to cook the dish. It will take about 40 minutes to cook. Turn on the oven to 375°F.

Hand Method: In a heavy saucepan, bring water, butter, and salt to a boil. When butter has melted, reduce heat, add flour all at once, and immediately start beating with a wooden spoon or spatula. Beat until dough forms a ball and comes away from the sides of the pan, and all flour is absorbed. Remove pan from the heat, and cool slightly. Make a well in center of dough and break an egg into it. Beat with a heavy wire whip to incorporate the egg into the dough. Repeat with the rest of the eggs, one at a time. Beat after each egg until ball of dough is smooth and glossy.

Food Processor Method: Follow procedure above up to the addition of eggs. Put ball of dough in processor, fitted with metal blade. Cover and process 5–10 seconds. Remove cover and break all four eggs into the bowl. Process until smooth and shiny, about 30–40 seconds. Mixture will be very thick.

Cover cheese with rounded tablespoons of dough. Do not smooth out top. Place in 375°F oven for 30–40 minutes, or until top is puffed, brown, and rigid (like a cream puff). Remove from the oven, prick the sides of the topping with the point of a small sharp knife to let out steam, and leave in the turned-off oven, with door ajar, for 10 minutes. Cut into 6 or 8 portions.

Seviche

1 pound fresh bay scallops

1 small onion, finely chopped

1 small green pepper, finely chopped

1 pimiento, chopped

1 teaspoon salt

⅛ teaspoon freshly ground black pepper

½ cup fresh lime juice, or ⅔ cup fresh lemon juice, or a combination

¼ cup olive oil

½ teaspoon thyme

2–3 dashes of Tabasco

1 small garlic clove, minced

1 avocado, peeled, seeded, sliced (optional)

Mix together everything but avocado in a glass or porcelain bowl. Allow to stand for 4 hours in the refrigerator, or overnight, stirring gently occasionally.

Slice the avocado, if used, just before serving, and sprinkle with lime or lemon juice to prevent discoloration. Arrange attractively on top of scallops, and mix in gently at serving time.

Apricot-Horseradish Purée

1 package (11 ounces) dried
    apricots (about 2 cups)
3 cups water

2 tablespoons sugar, or to taste
1 tablespoon horseradish,
    or to taste

Place apricots in a saucepan with the water. Cook gently, uncovered, for 8–10 minutes, or until apricots are soft. Add sugar and purée in a food mill, blender, or food processor. Do not overpurée; leave a little texture. Stir in horseradish. If a thinner sauce is desired, thin with a little water. Serve at room temperature or warmed.

CHICKEN AND TURKEY

Chicken, Rice, and Asparagus Hollandaise   *6 servings*

This is a beautiful assemblage of simple, good things, in which the pound of "meat" is chicken. Rather than being stretched by the other elements, the chicken is a delicious extra taste and texture. Served on a platter, the affair consists of a layer of rice strewn with strips of chicken breast browned in butter, a layer of asparagus, and a luscious topping of hollandaise sauce, foamy with the addition of beaten egg whites.

This is the kind of dish that has to be done at the last minute. If you have a big enough kitchen, it would be nice to have your guests with you there, munching on something with their drinks while you cook. Bread sticks, for instance, with a big tray of Italian cheeses would keep them busy. Cheeses to choose from are Fontina, Bel Paese, Provolone, and Taleggio.

Wine doesn't go very well with asparagus, but a big bottle of Soave or some other dry Italian white would be pleasantly thirst-quenching. Dessert could be as rich and fattening as you like.

Experienced cooks won't need a recipe for this. Here are directions for them, and a complete recipe follows for those who want it.

Cook 1½ cups rice in 3 cups chicken broth, with a pinch of thyme. Keep warm on a platter.

Cut 2 whole boneless, skinless chicken breasts (about 1 pound) into 12 strips. Cook them in 2 tablespoons butter until lightly brown, about 4 minutes. Place on top of the rice. Rinse the pan with ¼ cup dry Vermouth and pour over chicken and rice.

Cook enough asparagus for 6 until barely tender. Drain and place on top of chicken and rice.

Make a 3-egg hollandaise (this may be done ahead and kept warm). Beat the whites of the 3 eggs until stiff and mix gently with the hollandaise. Pour over the asparagus and serve immediately.

Hollandaise Sauce

3 egg yolks
1 tablespoon cold water
¼ pound butter (1 stick) at
    room temperature
¼ teaspoon salt, *only* if sweet
    butter is used, otherwise wait
    and see if it is needed

pinch of white pepper
2 tablespoons lemon juice
3 egg whites

The hollandaise can be made first and kept warm. The egg whites can be beaten while the asparagus cooks, and folded in at the last minute. The hollandaise will not be hot—it never is—but the freshly cooked asparagus will warm it enough.

Beat egg yolks in a stainless steel bowl until thick and light yellow. Add water to a saucepan and place bowl over, but not touching, barely simmering water. Stir and heat until warm, not hot, and beginning to thicken.

Add a tablespoon of butter and stir until it melts. Continue adding butter bit by bit, beating with a wire whip, until all butter is used. Don't add new butter until previous addition has melted and been incorporated. When butter is all in, cook and stir 2–3 minutes, until sauce thickens enough to coat a spoon. Set the bowl on a counter and stir in salt if needed, pepper, and lemon juice. Keep warm by placing bowl in another utensil containing lukewarm water.

Rice

1½ cups rice
   3 cups canned chicken broth,
      including fat on top

pinch of thyme

Put rice into boiling broth with the thyme. Bring to a boil again, stir once, cover, and turn down heat. Simmer for 20 minutes, or until rice is tender and liquid absorbed. Fluff with a fork onto a warm platter. Keep warm in 200°F oven.

Chicken

2 whole boneless, skinless
   chicken breasts, about
   1 pound

2 tablespoons butter
¼ cup dry Vermouth

Take off the long strip of chicken (the fillet or suprême) from each side of each breast. Cut the rest of each breast in 2 long pieces to more or less match the fillet. Trim off tendons. You should now have 12 strips of chicken.

In a heavy skillet, large enough to take all the strips without crowding, heat butter until it stops foaming. Put in chicken, season with salt and pepper, and cook, turning once, until chicken is lightly browned—about 4 minutes altogether. Spread chicken over rice, rinse pan with Vermouth, and pour over chicken. Keep warm.

Asparagus

Buy asparagus according to the number of stalks you want to serve to each person. Break off each stem at the point where it will break, not bend. I like to soak asparagus in tepid salted water for about 10 minutes to be sure no gritty dirt remains after washing. Peel stems down to the palest green (makes them edible to the very end), and plunge into boiling salted water in a wide, shallow pan. Cook until tender but not limp. It is done when it bows or dips slightly at each end when picked up with tongs in the middle. Drain and place over chicken and rice. Keep warm.

Finish

Beat egg whites until they stand in peaks. Fold a small amount of hollandaise into egg whites, then gently mix in the rest. Pour over asparagus and serve immediately.

Penny's Chicken Risotto   *6–8 servings*

Like many good dishes, this one happened because of a need to stretch ingredients on hand to feed unexpected guests. It has three elements: Each is cooked in its own utensil with its own seasonings, and then all three are combined. Freshly grated Parmesan cheese is stirred in at the end, not only for flavor, but to achieve the degree of moistness or dryness desired. If one of the utensils used is a handsome flameproof skillet or casserole that can be brought to the table, the need for still another dish for serving is eliminated. Here the rice is cooked in a casserole large enough to accommodate all three elements when they are done, and presentable enough to be brought to the table. Served piping hot, with a sprinkle of parsley down the middle or stirred in, the risotto needs only crusty bread and a salad of greens with the crisp touch of radishes and cucumbers to go with it.

Red or white wine would go with the meal: a Chardonnay or Muscadet for white; Rioja or Chianti Classico for red.

2½- to 3-quart lidded, flameproof casserole and 2 large, heavy skillets

Part 1
3 cups chicken broth   1½ cups rice

Part 2
2 whole boneless, skinless   2 garlic cloves, minced
   chicken breasts (about   salt and freshly ground black
   1 pound), in 1–2-inch pieces   pepper
2 tablespoons olive oil   1 teaspoon curry powder
2 medium onions, finely
   chopped

Part 3
 1 tablespoon olive oil   salt and freshly ground
¾ pound mushrooms, thinly   black pepper
   sliced   ½–¾ cup freshly grated
 4 ripe tomatoes (in season),   Parmesan cheese
   chopped, or 1 can (1 pound)   ¼ cup finely chopped parsley
   Italian tomatoes, mashed or
   chopped, liquid reserved

Part 1

In the flameproof casserole, bring the chicken broth to a boil, and stir in the rice. Bring to a simmer on low heat, cover, and cook for 20 minutes or until rice is done.

Part 2

While the rice is cooking, heat the oil in a large, heavy skillet and cook the onions and garlic over medium heat, stirring, until onions are limp but not brown. Turn up the heat and add the chicken pieces. Cook, stirring, until chicken has lost its pink color and is springy to the touch—about 4 minutes. Sprinkle with salt, pepper, and curry powder during cooking.

Part 3

In another heavy skillet, heat the oil and lightly sauté the mushrooms for about 1 minute. Add the tomatoes and cook, stirring, for 1–2 minutes, or until hot. Add salt and pepper to taste. Mixture will be moist with juices from the vegetables.

Stir the chicken mixture into the rice, when it is done, then the tomato mixture. Stir in Parmesan cheese a little at a time until mixture is as moist or dry as you want it. Sprinkle with parsley or stir it in, and serve on heated plates.

Turkey Breast and Eggplant Parmigiano   *6–8 servings*

If you serve spaghetti with garlic butter (recipe follows), good bread, salad, and fruit with this already sumptuous affair, even teenagers may be satisfied.

For the grown-ups, serve a hearty red wine that won't be overwhelmed by the rich tomato sauce in the Parmigiano—Rioja, Premiat, Chianti, or Zinfandel.

2½-quart baking dish (13 by 9 by 2 inches, approximately)

Sauce

1 tablespoon olive oil
1 medium onion, finely
    chopped (1 cup)
1 garlic clove, minced

1 can (2 pounds, 3 ounces)
    Italian tomatoes
½ teaspoon salt
¼ teaspoon pepper

Heat oil in a saucepan and cook onion and garlic in it until onion is limp and transparent. Add tomatoes and salt and pepper and simmer for 20 minutes.

Turkey and Eggplant

1 pound boneless, skinless turkey breast

2 medium eggplants, about 1 pound each, shiny, firm, unspotted, flat rather than dimpled on the bottom, long rather than squat, if possible

1 tablespoon butter, more as needed

1 tablespoon oil, more as needed

salt, pepper, oregano

¼ cup unseasoned bread crumbs

3 tablespoons freshly grated Parmesan cheese

3 tablespoons butter for turkey breast

salt, pepper, thyme

4–6 ounces Muenster cheese, sliced on cheese grater

If turkey breast is already in slices, pound the slices lightly between pieces of waxed paper to make them somewhat uniform in thickness. If breast is in one piece, freeze slightly, lay flat and slice through horizontally, as thinly as possible. Pound as above. Cut slices into 1½- to 2-inch pieces. Set aside.

Wash eggplants, trim off ends, and cut in ½-inch slices without peeling. In a large, heavy skillet, heat one tablespoon butter and one of oil. When butter stops foaming, cook a few of the slices very briefly, until there are odd spots of brown. Sprinkle with salt, pepper, and oregano as they cook. Set to drain on paper towels. Repeat with the rest of the eggplant, using more butter and oil as needed, never letting the slices sit too long in the pan.

Oil a baking dish or au gratin dish, and sprinkle with 1 tablespoon crumbs. Mix rest of crumbs with Parmesan cheese. Fit half the cooked eggplant on the bottom of the baking dish, and sprinkle with half the crumb and cheese mixture. Spread half the sauce on top.

Wipe skillet clean and heat the 3 tablespoons butter. When it stops foaming, put in turkey-breast pieces and cook until they feel firm to the touch and are browned in spots—under 4 minutes altogether. Sprinkle with salt, pepper, and thyme as they cook. Scatter as evenly as possible over sauce.

Cover turkey pieces with the rest of the eggplant and sprinkle with remaining crumb and Parmesan mixture, then the rest of the sauce. Scatter sliced Muenster on top and bake in preheated 400°F oven for 10–15 minutes, until hot and bubbling, and cheese has melted.

Garlic Butter (or Oil)

> 12 tablespoons butter (1½ sticks)
>   or ¾ cup olive oil
>   4 cloves garlic
> ½–1 teaspoon red-pepper flakes,
>   to taste
>
> salt and pepper
> ½ cup finely chopped parsley

Heat butter or oil in a small saucepan. Add garlic cloves, flattened with the flat of a big knife, pepper flakes, salt and pepper to taste. Let it cook over low heat for 2–3 minutes, without letting garlic brown. Discard garlic and toss the sauce with spaghetti and parsley. For 1 pound of spaghetti.

Chicken on Broccoli-and-Scallion Purée   *6 servings*

Glamorous enough for company, but not too exotic for the family, this handsome dish is one you will want in your repertoire. Browned strips of chicken breast lie on a pale green purée of broccoli and scallions, mixed with sour cream. It is topped with a buttery sprinkle of parsley and capers, and accented with the bright red of pimientos.

Suggestions for the rest of the meal: Cherry tomatoes heated in butter, with salt, pepper, and a sprinkle of ground ginger; green salad with some crisp vegetables and a few sliced raw mushrooms; for dessert, a big rich chocolate cake.

Red or white wine goes with this, light or full-bodied—a light dry Rioja Clarete or Tinto; a fine Burgundy like a Volnay for red, a Meursault for white; or try California Cabernets or Chardonnays.

2-quart baking dish (12 by 8 by 2 inches, approximately)

2 whole boneless, skinless
   chicken breasts, about
   1 pound
2 bunches broccoli
6 bunches scallions
6 tablespoons butter

¼ cup sour cream
   salt and white pepper to taste
½ cup finely chopped parsley
3 tablespoons drained capers
1–2 tablespoons drained, chopped
   pimientos

Take off the long strip of chicken (the fillet) from each side of each breast. Cut the rest of each side of each breast into 2 long pieces to more or less match the fillet. Trim off tendons. You should now have 12 strips of chicken. Set aside.

Wash broccoli and cut flowerets into uniform size, including the small stems. (Save large, heavy stems for other uses.) Cook in large quantity of boiling, salted water for 5 minutes. Drain at once.

Coarsely chop the scallions, using all the green tops that are crisp and fresh. Cook in 2 quarts of boiling, salted water for 3–5 minutes, or until white parts are just tender, but not soft. Drain well.

Purée vegetables through a food mill in batches, or in a food processor, also in batches. To keep a little texture, do not overprocess. Mix the batches together, and stir in 2 tablespoons of the butter, the sour cream, and ¼ cup of the parsley. Season to taste with salt and pepper. Spread the purée evenly in a buttered baking dish.

Heat 3 tablespoons of the butter in a heavy skillet, large enough to take the chicken without crowding. Put in the chicken strips, season with salt and pepper, and cook, turning once, until chicken is lightly browned—about 4 minutes altogether. Place chicken strips neatly over the purée so that each of 6 servings will have 2 pieces of chicken.

Heat remaining tablespoon of butter in the skillet with the rest of the parsley and the capers. Cook, stirring, a few seconds, and pour over chicken. Place in preheated 350°F oven for 10–20 minutes, or just long enough for purée to get hot. Serve sprinkled with pimientos.

Chicken on Green-Pea Purée   *6 servings*

Prepared in a similar fashion, and equally good-looking, this dish is similar to the preceding one, Chicken on Broccoli-and-Scallion Purée, with the vegetable the chief difference. Also, green peppercorns and dry Vermouth replace capers and parsley as a finish.

Hot buttered rutabaga in cubes, or carrots, cooked whole, would supply a fine touch of color with the bright green of the purée. Salad of endive and beets would supply crispness and more color.

This calls for a soft and fruity white wine, Vouvray or Sancerre from the Loire, Riesling or Sylvaner from Alsace or the Rhineland, Chenin Blanc or Sémillon from California.

2-quart baking dish (12 by 8 by 2 inches, approximately)

2 whole boneless, skinless chicken breasts, about 1 pound	¼ cup finely chopped parsley salt and pepper
4 teaspoons *crumbled* dried mint	½ teaspoon thyme
2 cups chopped scallions	2 teaspoons green peppercorns, drained
4 packages frozen peas	⅓ cup dry Vermouth
8 tablespoons butter (1 stick)	2 hard-boiled eggs, peeled and finely chopped
½ cup sour cream	

Take off the long strip of chicken (the fillet) from each breast. Cut the rest of each side of each breast into 2 long pieces to more or less match the fillet. Trim off tendons. You should now have 12 strips of chicken. Set aside.

In large lidded saucepan, bring a cup of salted water to a boil and put in mint and scallions. Add frozen peas. Cook on high heat, gently breaking up clusters of peas. Turn down heat, cover, and cook on low heat until peas are cooked and hot, but not mushy. Drain.

Purée vegetables through a food mill in batches, or in a processor, also in batches. To keep a little texture, do not overprocess. Mix the batches together and stir in 4 tablespoons of the butter, the sour cream, and parsley. Season to taste with salt and pepper. Spread the purée evenly in a buttered baking dish.

Heat 3 tablespoons of the butter in a heavy skillet, large enough to take the chicken without crowding. When the butter stops foaming, put in the chicken strips. Season with salt, pepper, and thyme, and cook, turning once, until chicken is lightly browned—about 4 minutes altogether. Place chicken strips neatly over the purée so that each of 6 servings will have 2 pieces of chicken.

Heat remaining tablespoon of butter in the skillet with green peppercorns. Pour Vermouth into pan and cook, stirring, until wine has cooked down to about half. Pour over chicken. Place in preheated 350°F oven for 10–20 minutes, or just long enough for purée to get hot. Serve decorated with chopped egg—down the middle and across, on the purée only, for instance.

2. The Glamour
Treatment — Pastry

PHYLLO PASTRY

Meat mixtures enclosed in layers of buttered, tissue-thin phyllo sheets make wonderful party fare—impressive and good to eat. Packaged phyllo can be found in some supermarkets now, refrigerated or frozen, so popular has it become, but you may have to search it out in Greek neighborhoods. It comes in one-pound packages of 16- by 22-inch (approximately) sheets, a vast number of them.

The only thing that might be called difficult about using phyllo sheets is that you have to work quickly with one sheet at a time, getting it buttered before it dries, and keeping all the rest well covered until they are needed. Leftover sheets, carefully wrapped, can be refrigerated for a few days, and frozen for longer. Be sure the phyllo is thoroughly defrosted before attempting to peel off a sheet.

Lamb and Onion Pie   *8–10 servings*

No doubt in Greece, where this dish comes from, it would be made with leeks, so when leeks are cheap and readily available, by all means use them if you can. It is a fine dish as given here but you can use some leeks along with the onions or scallions if you like. I happen to resent having a vegetable cost more than the meat in a dish, as leeks can do in New York. Instructions for preparing leeks follow the recipe, which otherwise remains the same.

70

A big, leafy salad with a little feta cheese and some black olives in it would go well with the pie, and a fruit salad of oranges and bananas with a sprinkle of kirsch and sugar makes a pleasant dessert.

A fine Bordeaux or Burgundy red—an Hermitage or Côte Rôtie from France; from Italy a Barolo or Gattinara—any good red wine suits this dish.

3-quart baking dish (14 by 10 by 2 inches, approximately)

Cream Sauce

3 tablespoons butter
3 tablespoons flour

3 cups milk
1 teaspoon salt

Melt butter, blend in the flour, remove from the heat, and stir in the milk and salt. When the sauce is smooth, put back on the heat and cook, stirring, until it boils and thickens to a creamy consistency. Set aside to cool. Stir occasionally as it cools to keep a skin from forming.

Lamb and Onion Mixture

2 tablespoons butter
3 cups finely chopped onion, or
   scallions with all fresh, crisp
   green parts
2 garlic cloves, minced
1 pound lean ground lamb
¼ cup dry white wine
¼ teaspoon cinnamon

½ teaspoon nutmeg
½ teaspoon white pepper
1 teaspoon salt

1 cup Parmesan cheese, freshly
   grated
4 eggs, beaten

In a large, heavy skillet, melt one tablespoon of the butter and put in the onions and garlic. Cook over low heat, stirring, until the onions are soft and pale gold, but not brown. Remove from the skillet and set aside in a bowl.

Crumble the meat into the same skillet with the other tablespoon of butter. Breaking up the chunks with a fork, cook over fairly high heat until the meat begins to brown and the pieces are the same size. Pour off any fat from the pan. Add the wine and seasonings and cook over low heat until the wine has evaporated. Combine with the onions and garlic and remove from the heat.

Mix the cheese with the cream sauce, and add the well-beaten eggs when the sauce is at room temperature. Fold the meat and onion mixture into the cream sauce, cheese, and egg combination.

Assembly

    1 pound phyllo pastry (leftover
        can be frozen, well wrapped)
    ¼ pound butter (1 stick),
        more if needed
    2 tablespoons olive oil

Spread out the phyllo pastry, cut the sheets in half the short way for easier handling, and cover immediately with a damp cloth. Keep covered while you work, uncovering only to take up a sheet of pastry. Refrigerate half the pastry, well wrapped, until needed.

In a small saucepan, melt the butter and add the oil. Keep warm but do not boil. Using a brush, lightly coat the bottom and sides of a baking pan with the butter-and-oil mixture. Lay a sheet of pastry in the pan, with excess hanging over one end and one side. Brush with butter and oil. Fold in the excess to fit bottom of pan and brush with butter and oil. Repeat until 12 sheets have been used, alternating the sides and ends that the excess hangs over.

Spread the mixture of meat, onions, sauce, and eggs over the pastry evenly, and cover with 12 more sheets, each brushed with the butter and oil and fitted to the pan as before. After buttering the top layer, score the pastry with a sharp knife, not quite through to the filling. Score once down the middle the long way, and 3 or 4 times across to make 8 or 10 servings. Sprinkle with a few drops of water, and place in a preheated 375°F oven for 45–60 minutes, until puffed and golden.

To Use Leeks

Buy 2½ pounds. Trim off roots, bad outer leaves, and the green tops down to just the palest green. Split lengthwise and clean under running water, carefully spreading the leaves to remove dirt. Cut across in fine slices.

Beef and Spinach Pie *8–10 servings*

Tomatoes in some form would supply a pleasant moistness for this hearty pie in its flaky phyllo pastry. In season, plain sliced tomatoes with fresh basil and a squeeze of lemon would do the trick. Another time of the year, zucchini or eggplant, lightly sautéed in olive oil, in a tomato sauce would be good. A first course could be jellied or hot consommé, appetite-stirring but not too heavy. For dessert, sherbet or ice cream with a dollop of liqueur poured over.

Beer suits this spinach pie, but the daring might like the resinous Greek wine called Retsina.

3-quart baking dish (14 by 10 by 2 inches, approximately)

Step 1

1½ pounds fresh spinach, or	½ teaspoon salt
2 packages frozen spinach	¼ teaspoon white pepper
1 tablespoon olive oil	¼ teaspoon nutmeg
2 bunches scallions, chopped	

Wash, trim off heavy stems, drain, and chop fresh spinach. Defrost, squeeze, and drain frozen spinach.

Heat the oil in a heavy pot, large enough to take the spinach, and lightly sauté the scallions until they are limp. Add the spinach and cook over low heat, stirring, until moisture has evaporated. Add salt, pepper, and nutmeg.

Step 2

1 tablespoon olive oil	¼ teaspoon white pepper
1 pound lean ground beef	1 teaspoon oregano
¾ teaspoon salt	

In a heavy skillet, heat the oil and crumble in the meat. Cook, stirring and breaking up lumps, until the pieces are uniform in size and beginning to brown. Add salt, pepper, and oregano, and pour off any accumulated fat. Mix with spinach and scallion mixture.

Step 3

5 eggs	¼ cup chopped fresh dill, or
½ pound feta cheese	1 teaspoon dried dill
1 pound (16 ounces) cottage	2 tablespoons lemon juice
cheese	

In a large bowl, beat the eggs well. Crumble the feta cheese into the eggs. Stir in the cottage cheese, dill, and lemon juice. Combine with the meat and spinach mixture.

Step 4

1 pound phyllo pastry   2 tablespoons olive oil
   (leftover can be frozen)
12 tablespoons butter (1½ sticks),
   more if needed

Spread out the phyllo pastry, cut the sheets in half the short way, and immediately cover with a damp cloth. Keep covered while you work, uncovering only to take up a sheet of pastry.

In a small saucepan, melt the butter and add the oil. Keep warm but do not allow to boil. Using a brush, lightly coat the bottom and sides of a baking pan with the butter-and-oil mixture. Lay a sheet of pastry in the pan, with excess hanging over one end and one side. Brush with butter-and-oil mixture. Fold in the excess to fit bottom of pan and brush with butter and oil. Repeat until 12 sheets have been used, alternating the sides and ends that the excess hangs over.

Spread the meat, spinach, cheese, and egg mixture over the pastry evenly, and cover with 12 more sheets, each brushed with the butter and oil and fitted to the pan as before. After buttering the top layer, score the pastry with a sharp knife, not quite through to the filling. Score once down the middle the long way and three or four times across, to make 8 or 10 servings. Sprinkle with a few drops of water, and place in a preheated 375°F oven for 25–30 minutes, or until puffed and golden.

Meat Triangles in Phyllo   *8 servings*

Asparagus or broccoli in season, with lemon and butter, if hollandaise seems too rich, would go well with these flavorful filled pastries. A salad of tomatoes, green pepper, and onion rings, with a few capers in the dressing, makes a good moist and piquant accent.

Jug wines, chilled—red, white, or pink—are suggested for this. Add a wedge of lemon and ice cubes to the wine.

Cook on a baking sheet

1 tablespoon butter
2 strips bacon, diced
1 large garlic clove, minced
1 medium zucchini, chopped in ¼-inch pieces
1 medium onion, finely chopped
1 pound lean ground beef
1¼ teaspoons salt
½ teaspoon freshly ground black pepper
1¼ teaspoons oregano

1 tablespoon grated lemon rind
2 tablespoons flour
2 tablespoons freshly grated Parmesan cheese
⅓ cup milk
1 tablespoon lemon juice

about ½ pound phyllo pastry (phyllo comes in 1-pound packages; freeze excess)
¼ pound butter, melted but not boiled

Put the butter and diced bacon into a large, heavy skillet and cook, stirring to break up the clusters of bacon pieces, until bacon is golden brown. Add the garlic, zucchini, and onions, and cook until onions are slightly soft. Crumble in the ground beef and cook, stirring and breaking up lumps, until meat loses its red color.

Stir in salt, pepper, oregano, and lemon rind. Sprinkle flour over the mixture and stir until no white shows. Stir in Parmesan cheese. Add milk, stir, and cook 10–15 minutes, until mixture is thick but not dry. Stir in lemon juice. Allow mixture to cool.

Open the phyllo pastry carefully, and cut off 6 inches of the pile of sheets with scissors. The sheets come about 16 inches wide and 22 inches long, so make your cut across the short way, giving you a pile of sheets 6 by 16 inches. Cover all the pastry, including the 6-inch strips, with plastic and a dampened towel.

On a long piece of waxed paper, lay out 1 6-inch sheet of phyllo pastry. With a brush, paint the whole strip with warm melted butter. Place 2 more sheets neatly on top, buttering each completely. Keep the rest of the pastry covered.

Place one eighth of the cooled meat mixture in a triangle on the buttered pastry, starting at lower left corner. Meat should go 5¾ inches up left side, straight across to right side, and diagonally from there back to left hand corner. Lift all three layers at bottom right corner and fold over meat mixture so that bottom edges lie along left side. Be sure all corners have meat in them. Butter the top, and fold up; butter and fold to the right; butter and fold up again. Butter the top and bring the last piece of pastry over to cover. After a last brush of butter, press lightly to fasten down. Don't worry if it doesn't come out evenly as long as two sides are about 6" long and meat is fully enclosed.

Place on an unbuttered cookie sheet and repeat the procedure with 6" strips until you have 8 triangles. Cut more strips if needed. Do not set triangles too close together, better to use 2 sheets than to crowd them.

Sprinkle each triangle with a few drops of cold water, and place in a preheated 400°F oven for 12–15 minutes or until puffed and golden.

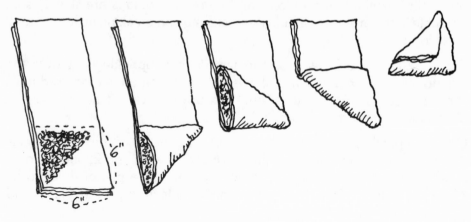

PASTRY-COVERED LOAVES AND LARGE TURNOVERS

Pastry not only makes meat go further, it makes a dinner into an occasion. Two loaves, with the pastry applied in different ways, and one large turnover follow, and a recipe for their pastry. Of course you can use your own, based on 2¼ or 2½ cups of flour.

These loaves and the turnover need to be cut in wide slices, an inch or so, because the pastry falls apart. It does that no matter how you slice, to some extent, but I don't think it matters. It helps if you allow them to cool for a few minutes before carving. They are not the sort of dishes that have to be piping hot. They are good cold, too, and are much easier to slice.

Pastry for Loaves and Large Turnovers

2¼ cups flour
¾ teaspoon salt
10 tablespoons butter in ½-inch
    pieces, cold
2 tablespoons vegetable
    shortening, cold

1 tablespoon lemon juice
5 tablespoons ice water, ¼–½
    tablespoon more if needed
    for ball to form
1 egg beaten with 1 tablespoon
    milk, for glaze

Hand Method: Mix together flour and salt. With 2 knives or pastry blender, cut in the butter and shortening until mixture is like coarse meal. Add lemon juice and water, mixing lightly with hands until dough forms into a ball. Use a little more if needed to incorporate all the flour. Dust with flour, smooth over cracks, wrap in plastic, and refrigerate until filling is made.

Food processor method: With steel blade in place, put flour, salt, butter, and shortening into work bowl, and process until mixture resembles coarse meal. With the machine running, pour in lemon juice and water, and process until dough forms a ball. Take out the dough, dust with flour, smooth the surface, wrap in plastic, and refrigerate until needed.

Ham and Rice Loaf in Pastry   6 servings

Beautiful in its golden wrappings of pastry, this loaf sandwiches ham between layers of rice, cheese, and a creamy sauce. The ham is marinated to give it extra taste, and the marinade is added to the rice to carry the flavors through. Serve with a small bowl of sour cream mixed with Dijon mustard to taste.

The loaf, surrounded by watercress or parsley sprigs, could be accompanied by just a big green salad. For a more formal meal, or a more filling one, it could be preceded by a light soup and served with broccoli or green beans, the salad then following as a separate course.

A German Kabinett wine from the Rhine or the Moselle, less apt to be sweet than some, goes with the loaf; or perhaps something drier, like a Chardonnay.

Cook on an edged cookie sheet

1 recipe Pastry for Loaves and
　　Large Turnovers

1 pound cooked ham in ¼-inch
　　dice
½ cup Amontillado Sherry
¼ cup finely chopped shallots
　　or scallions
¼ cup finely chopped parsley
⅛ teaspoon each allspice, salt

¼ teaspoon each thyme, white
　　pepper
3 cups cold cooked rice (1 cup
　　rice cooked in 2 cups
　　chicken broth)
2 cups velouté sauce
　　(recipe follows)
4–6 ounces thinly sliced Jarlsberg
　　or Gruyère cheese

Put the ham in a nonmetallic bowl with the Sherry, shallots or scallions, parsley, and seasonings. Allow to stand for at least one hour, stirring occasionally. When you are ready to use the ham, drain it, and stir the marinade into the rice.

Velouté Sauce

4 tablespoons butter	2 tablespoons Amontillado
4 tablespoons flour	Sherry
1½ cups canned or fresh chicken broth	½ cup heavy cream
	salt and pepper to taste

In a heavy saucepan, melt butter and stir in flour to make a smooth paste. Remove from heat and whisk in chicken broth. When mixture is smooth, put back on heat and cook, stirring constantly, until it comes to a boil. Cook on low heat, stirring, until sauce thickens. Stir in Sherry and cream. Add salt and pepper to taste. Allow to cool.

Assembly

Lightly butter an edged cookie sheet. Divide pastry into 3 sections. Roll out 1 section and trim to 7 by 14 inches. Drape over rolling pin and unroll onto the cookie sheet. Spread half the rice over pastry, leaving a 1½-inch border all around. Sprinkle lightly with salt and pepper. Carefully spoon half the velouté sauce over rice, then half the cheese. Gently flatten the cheese and spread the ham over it. Cover with the rest of the cheese, then the rest of the velouté sauce, and top with remaining rice. Brush edges of pastry with egg glaze.

Roll out remaining pastry and trim to 9 by 16 inches. Drape over rolling pin and unroll over loaf. Press edges together and trim to about 1 inch around loaf. Press edges with tines of a fork, or make diagonal scorings with the back of a knife, being careful not to make holes.

Cut two holes in top of loaf, about ½ inch in diameter. Decorate holes with little doughnuts of pastry, and the rest of the loaf with strips, circles, or leaf shapes, all fastened on with glaze. Feel free, any decoration looks fine when it comes out of the oven. Paint entire loaf with glaze after decorating.

Place loaf in bottom third of preheated 400°F oven for 20 minutes. Bake for 25 minutes more at 375°F, in upper third of oven. Allow to stand for 10–15 minutes before serving.

Beef Turnover

6–8 servings

This handsome turnover is Scandinavian enough to provide a nice excuse for a simple Scandinavian-style dinner.

Before the main course, with aquavit, you could serve black bread with Crèma Dania cheese, and cucumbers in a sweet-sour dill sauce (recipe given); with the loaf, spinach, and a relish-salad accent of pickled beets with thinly sliced red onions and a sprinkle of ground cloves—and beer to drink.

For dessert, something with apples—baked apples, say, since the oven is being used anyway.

1 recipe Pastry for Loaves and
    Large Turnovers

2 tablespoons butter
¼ cup finely chopped onion
1 large boiled potato, mashed
    (1 cup)
1 pound lean ground beef, or
    ½ pound ground beef and
    ½ pound lean ground lamb
¼ cup finely chopped parsley
2 tablespoons fine, dry bread
    crumbs (unseasoned)

1 egg
1¼ teaspoons salt
½ teaspoon white pepper
1 tablespoon chopped fresh dill,
    or 1 teaspoon dried dill
½ teaspoon marjoram
½ cup grated sharp Cheddar
    cheese
½ cup milk

fresh dill stalks, watercress, or
    parsley sprigs for garnish

In a small skillet, heat the butter and cook the onion until it is limp and transparent, but not brown. In a large mixing bowl, combine the onions and their butter, the mashed potato, beef (or beef and lamb), parsley, and bread crumbs.

Lightly beat the egg in a measuring cup and add the salt, pepper, dill, and marjoram. Combine thoroughly with meat mixture. Stir in the cheese, add the milk, and mix again.

Assembly
Roll out the pastry to a rectangle, 12 by 16 inches. Save the trimmings for decoration. Form the meat mixture into a loaf about 8 by 10 inches, and place on one half of the pastry, leaving a 1-inch border all around. Paint the border with water and bring up the other half of the pastry to cover the meat. Press the edges together and crimp with fingers or fork. Cut off excess pastry, but be sure there are no holes or cracks.

Make three ½-inch holes along the top of the turnover, and trim with ¼-inch strips or rolls of pastry, fastened on with the egg glaze. Now paint the whole top and sides of the pastry with glaze and have fun with decorations. Rounds, leaf shapes, diagonal strips, stems and flowers—all look marvelous when the turnover comes out of the oven. Paint decorations with egg glaze.

With the help of a couple of spatulas, ease the turnover onto a lightly floured edged cookie sheet, and place in lower third of preheated 400°F oven for 20 minutes. Turn oven to 375°F and cook another 20–25 minutes in upper third of oven, until nicely browned. Allow to stand for 10 minutes before serving, surrounded by parsley, watercress, or fresh dill.

Sweet-Sour Cucumbers

3 medium cucumbers
   salted water to cover
     (½ teaspoon salt per cup)
⅔ cup cider vinegar
½ cup water
½ teaspoon salt

2 tablespoons sugar
¼ teaspoon freshly ground black
   pepper
2 tablespoons chopped fresh dill,
   or 1½ teaspoons dried dill,
   if you must

Cut off the ends of the cucumbers and peel them. Cut them in half lengthwise and scoop out the seeds. Cut the halves across the middle, slice the quarters lengthwise into 6 strips. Put the slices in salted water to stand in the refrigerator for an hour.

Pour off the salted water and add the rest of the ingredients. Chill for 2–3 hours, stirring occasionally. Drain just before serving, decorated with sprigs of fresh dill.

Beef Loaf in Pastry   *6 servings*

Mushrooms in a Madeira sauce (recipe given) make a vegetable and sauce combined for this pastry-covered loaf. All that is needed then is a salad— tomatoes and scallions, say, with lemon in the dressing and a touch of basil—to complete the main course. Add a green vegetable if appetites warrant, and finish with fruit in season.

White or red wine, light and young, goes with the loaf.

1 recipe Pastry for Loaves and
Large Turnovers

1 pound lean ground beef
3–4 slices firm stale bread, crusts
removed
2 tablespoons finely chopped
parsley
1 egg
1 large garlic clove mashed with
1 teaspoon salt

2 tablespoons tomato paste
mixed with 3 tablespoons
water
⅛ teaspoon cayenne, or more to
taste
1 tablespoon chopped fresh
mint, or 2 teaspoons dried
mint
½ teaspoon coriander
½ teaspoon oregano
watercress or parsley for
garnish

In a mixing bowl, put the beef, the bread—torn into 1½ cups coarse crumbs, and the parsley. Lightly beat the egg in a small bowl and add the garlic mashed with salt, and all the other ingredients, except garnish. Add this mixture to the meat and mix thoroughly.

Assembly
Roll out pastry and trim to a rectangle, 15 by 10 inches. Lay meat down the center the long way, in a roll about 2½ inches in diameter, to within 2 inches of each end. Bring one long side of the pastry up over the meat, brush generously with egg glaze. Bring up the other long side of the pastry to cover, and press gently to seal. Pinch the ends together, using egg glaze to seal. Trim off excess pastry, but be sure there are no holes.

Make 3 evenly spaced holes, ½ inch in diameter, down the middle of the pastry. Trim the edges of the holes with strips of pastry fastened on with egg glaze. Cover the join on the top of the roll with circles, strips, rounds, or leaf shapes, fastened on with glaze. Decorate the whole loaf with any shapes you fancy—it all looks beautiful when it comes out of the oven.

Paint entire roll with glaze and place on a lightly buttered cookie sheet. Bake in lower third of preheated 400°F oven for 20 minutes. Turn oven down to 375°F and cook roll in upper third of the oven for another 25 minutes, until nicely browned.

Remove from oven and allow to stand for 10–15 minutes before serving, surrounded by watercress or parsley.

Mushrooms in Madeira Sauce
1¾ cups, plus mushrooms

3 tablespoons minced onion
⅓ cup Madeira
3 tablespoons butter
3 tablespoons flour
1¾ cups beef broth

½–¾ pound mushrooms, coarsely
   chopped, lightly sautéed in 1
   tablespoon butter
salt and pepper

In a heavy saucepan, cook onions with Madeira until wine has almost evaporated. Stir in butter, and, off the heat, stir in flour. With saucepan back on the heat, gradually add broth. Cook, stirring, until sauce boils and thickens. Season to taste with salt and pepper. Sprinkle salt and pepper on sautéed mushrooms and add to sauce.

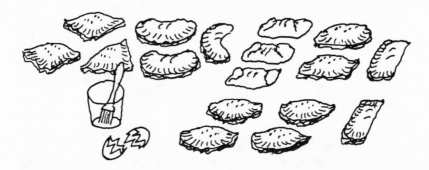

INDIVIDUAL TURNOVERS AND A DEEP-DISH PIE

Meat mixtures wrapped in pastry, from pasties to piroshki, are found all over the world. What makes them good—when they are good—is a combination of pastry that has taste and texture on its own, and a filling that stands up to it. I have found that the pastry I like best for these turnovers is a sour-cream one, whatever the filling. The fillings are designed for variety and strength of taste, without too much concern for ethnic authenticity.

A recipe for sour-cream pastry follows, and 3 fillings to go with it. Needless to say, you can use a pastry of your own, based on 2 cups of flour. For making, filling, and cooking the turnovers, follow the directions that come after the sour-cream pastry recipe.

Sour-Cream Pastry for Individual Turnovers

2 cups sifted flour
½ teaspoon salt
1 stick butter (¼ pound), in
    1-inch pieces
½–1 cup sour cream

2 tablespoons butter in ½-inch
    dabs
1 egg, lightly beaten with 1
    tablespoon milk, for glaze

Hand Method: Combine flour and salt. With 2 knives or pastry blender, cut in butter until mixture is like coarse meal. Stir in ½ cup sour cream, and keep adding more until dough can be formed into a ball. Dough will be moist. Dust with flour, flatten to 1 inch, smooth out cracks, and chill for 15–30 minutes, wrapped in plastic, until firm enough to roll out.

Food Processor Method: With steel blade in place, put flour, salt, and butter into work bowl, and process until mixture resembles coarse meal. Add ½ cup sour cream and process, adding more sour cream by table-spoons, until dough forms a ball. Dough will be moist. Remove and dust with flour. Flatten to 1 inch and smooth out cracks. Wrap in plastic and chill for 15–30 minutes, until firm enough to roll out.

On a floured board, roll out pastry to a 10-by-15-inch rectangle, 10-inch side toward you. Scatter the 2 tablespoons of butter dabs over the pastry. Fold dough over in thirds, give it a quarter turn, and roll out again to 10 by 15 inches. Fold in thirds. Repeat twice more, chilling between rollings. After last rolling, fold in thirds, dust with flour, wrap in plastic, and refrigerate until needed.

To Make, Fill, and Cook the Turnovers
Take pastry from the refrigerator and divide into 2 equal parts. Leaving one half in the refrigerator, roll out the other to a 12-by-12-inch square, and cut across and down to make four 6-by-6-inch squares. Spread the filling mixture on a platter, and score it to indicate the amount for 8 portions. Place a triangle of filling on one half of each of the 4 squares, leaving a ½-inch border around. Wet this border with water, and fold the empty side of the pastry over filling, pressing edges together with tines of a fork or the back of a knife, or make a wavy edge with the fingers. Prick holes in the top, paint with egg glaze, and place on a buttered, edged cookie sheet. Repeat with rest of pastry and filling. Place in preheated 375°F oven for 20 minutes, or until nicely brown.

Alternate Shapes
1. Round the points of triangles and arch the folded sides to make crescents.
2. Place filling down the middle of each square, leaving ½-inch margins at each end. Fold up one side over filling, brush edge with glaze, and bring up other side to cover. Press gently to seal. Seal ends with glaze and pinch together. Prick top with a fork.

3. Place filling on one half of squares, with ½-inch margins. Wet margins with water, and bring up other side to make 3-by-6-inch rectangles. Press edges together, decorate with fork or knife, and prick holes on top.

4. Make circles out of the squares, and fold over to make half circles. Make a ½-inch hole in each top, and use scraps to make little flat doughnut shapes around holes.

Empanadas   8 servings of 1 turnover each

Serve with just a salad and Mexican-style yellow rice (recipe given). For those who like rice and beans in the same meal, the salad could be black beans in an oil-and-vinegar dressing with plenty of scallions. Garnish the plate with watercress or sprigs of parsley to supply some green.

Rioja or Chianti—or beer—is good to drink with the empanadas.

1 recipe Sour Cream Pastry

2 tablespoons olive oil, vegetable oil, or half and half
1 medium onion, finely chopped
½ medium green pepper, finely chopped
1 large garlic clove, minced
1 pound lean ground beef
1 can (1 pound) Italian tomatoes, drained and chopped, or 1½ cups fresh tomatoes, peeled and chopped

2 tablespoons chopped canned green chilies
1 teaspoon salt
¼ teaspoon pepper
1½ teaspoons cumin
2 tablespoons raisins, allowed to stand in boiling water for 10 minutes and drained
10 small, pitted green olives, chopped

Make pastry and refrigerate.

In a wide, heavy skillet or saucepan with a lid, heat the oil and add onions, green pepper, and garlic. Cook, stirring, until vegetables have softened. Crumble in the meat and cook, stirring and breaking up lumps, until it has lost its pink and begun to brown. Add remaining ingredients and cook until liquid has evaporated. Allow to cool, and pour off any fat that appears.

Fill and cook as described previously.

Mexican-Style Yellow Rice

2 tablespoons butter
1 small onion, finely chopped
    (½ cup)
1 small green pepper, finely
    chopped

1½ cups rice
2 cups water
1 cup tomato juice
1 jar (4 ounces) pimientos,
    coarsely chopped

Heat butter in a lidded saucepan. Put in onion, green pepper, and rice. Cook on low heat, stirring, until onions and peppers have softened slightly, and rice has turned opaque. Add water, tomato juice, and salt. Bring to a boil, stir once, and cover. Cook on low heat for 20 minutes, or until rice is tender and liquid has been absorbed. Add pimientos and fluff with a fork.

Piroshki

8 servings of 1 turnover each,
approximately 6 by 6 by 6 inches

Fresh dill is needed for the filling of these pastries and the sour cream, horseradish, and dill sauce that goes with them (recipe given).

Cauliflower or broccoli, cooked just until it is tender-crisp, and buttered, goes well with the piroshki. Beets with rings of red onion, or tomatoes with scallions, in oil and vinegar, would make colorful salad choices.

1 recipe Sour Cream Pastry

2 tablespoons butter
2 medium onions, finely chopped
    (about 2 cups)
1 pound lean ground beef
1¼ teaspoons salt

¼ teaspoon freshly ground black
    pepper
1 tablespoon flour, mixed with
    ½ cup water
¼ cup finely chopped fresh dill
2 hard-boiled eggs, finely
    chopped

Make pastry and refrigerate.

Melt the butter in a large, heavy skillet, and cook the onions until they are limp and transparent, but not brown. Crumble in the beef and cook, stirring and breaking up lumps, until it has lost its pink color. Add salt and pepper, and mash mixture until there are no chunks. Stir in flour and water and cook until bubbling and thickened, and liquid has cooked away but mixture is not dry. Stir in egg and dill. Allow to cool.

Fill and cook as described previously.

Sour Cream, Horseradish, and Dill Sauce

1½ cups sour cream
  3 tablespoons horseradish
  ¼ cup finely chopped fresh dill

¼ teaspoon salt
⅛ teaspoon white pepper

Mix all ingredients together, adding more salt and pepper if desired. Serve in a small bowl with a sprig of dill on top.

Individual Beef Turnovers   8 servings

There is plenty of taste in these turnovers, with bacon and sour cream in them, among other things. A simple mixed green salad with an oil-and-vinegar dressing—or a fancier one of endive, watercress, and fresh grape-fruit—would be good with the meal. An interesting vegetable dish that goes well with filled pastries is a purée of potatoes, carrots, and turnip (recipe given).

Dessert should be cool and simple—a fruit salad, if fruit has not been used in the salad, or a sherbet.

For wine, a Valpolicella, Rioja, or California Petite Sirah are suggested.

1 recipe Sour Cream Pastry

2 strips bacon, diced
1 tablespoon butter
2 tablespoons minced shallots
1 pound lean ground beef
1 tablespoon flour

1 teaspoon salt
¼ teaspoon freshly ground black
  pepper
¾ teaspoon oregano
¾ teaspoon dried basil
½ cup beef broth
½–¾ cup sour cream

In a large, heavy skillet, cook the bacon until it is golden, separating the bits with a fork as they cook. Add butter and shallots, and cook for a minute or two. Crumble in beef and cook, stirring and breaking up lumps, until no pink shows. Sprinkle in flour and stir until no white shows. Stir in seasoning and broth, clearing bottom of pan. Cook until thickened. Allow to cool and pour off any accumulated fat, blotting with paper towel to remove the last. Stir in sour cream to make mixture moist but not runny.

Fill and cook as described previously.

Turnip, Carrot, and Potato Purée

6 medium potatoes (1½ pounds),
  peeled and quartered
3 white turnips (¾ pound),
  peeled and halved
4 medium carrots (½ pound),
  peeled and halved

4 tablespoons butter
1 teaspoon salt
½ teaspoon freshly ground black
  pepper, more to taste
½–¾ teaspoon ground coriander

Cook the vegetables all together in boiling salted water until they are tender. Drain well and purée through a food mill or in food processor. Do not overprocess; leave a little texture. Stir in 3 tablespoons of the butter, salt, pepper, and coriander. Turn into a 2-quart baking dish or casserole, dot with remaining tablespoon of butter, and heat in preheated 350°F oven for 10–20 minutes, until purée is heated through.

Variation: Stir in some onions and green peppers, lightly sautéed in butter.

Goulash Deep-Dish Pie   *6 servings*

Hungarian goulash, with Viennese and Italian touches to make a strong, rich taste, is topped here with melt-in-the-mouth pastry. A big salad of greens and crisp vegetables, some strong cheeses to follow, and fresh fruit could round out the meal.

A flowery white wine, like an Austrian Riesling or Müller-Thurgau from Loiben or Krems, is good with this; so are hearty reds like Egri Bikavér from Hungary, or a French Rhône. To finish with a flourish, serve Viennese coffee and Kirsch.

10-inch pie pan, or 8–9-inch shallow 1-quart baking dish

1 recipe Pastry for Deep-Dish
  Pie (recipe follows)

1 pound boneless stewing beef,
  in ½-inch pieces
1 teaspoon marjoram
2 teaspoons finely minced zest of
  lemon (zest is rind without
  any white)
1 teaspoon caraway seeds

1 clove garlic, minced
¾ teaspoon salt
2 tablespoons butter
1 pound onions, chopped
4 teaspoons sweet Hungarian
  paprika
1 tablespoon tomato paste
2 tablespoons flour
⅔–1 cup water

Wipe and dry meat on paper towels. It is not to be browned but needs to be dry anyway. Crush or mash together the marjoram, lemon rind, caraway seeds, garlic, and salt.

In a heavy, lidded flameproof casserole—preferably a wide, shallow one—melt the butter and stir in the mashed seasonings. Add the onions and cook gently until they are limp and transparent. Sprinkle in the paprika. Stir to mix and cook for about 1 minute. Stir in the tomato paste.

Add beef, keeping a low flame under the casserole. Stir until meat is coated (not browned), and loses its raw red color. (It is hard to tell with everything so red, but you can.) Sprinkle in flour, stirring until it is absorbed. Add enough water to cover the bottom of the casserole well. The meat and onions supply some liquid.

Bring to a simmer and cover. The goulash may now be cooked on top of the stove or in a preheated 300–325°F oven (whatever temperature will maintain the simmer). Since there is very little liquid, you may find it less apt to stick to the pan if cooked in the oven. Either way, check occasionally and add a small quantity of hot water if needed. Cook for 45–60 minutes, or until meat is tender.

Tip pot and skim off fat. Turn mixture into pie pan, or baking dish. Roll out deep-dish pastry and trim to fit pan or dish, with ½-inch overhang. Fold in half, cut slits or decorative holes in the center, and place on the still-hot goulash. Open out to reach the other side of the pan. Fold excess pastry under and crimp the edge. Use scraps to make leaf shapes, rounds, or strips, and stick them on the pastry with the slightly beaten egg white. Don't worry about what you put on, any old shape looks handsome when it is cooked. Paint the whole pie with egg white, and cook 10 minutes in preheated 425°F oven, then about 20 minutes at 350°F, or until nicely browned.

Pastry for Deep-Dish Pie

 2 cups sifted flour
¾ teaspoon salt
⅔ cup lard or vegetable
    shortening, very cold

1 egg, separated
3 tablespoons water

Hand Method: Mix flour and salt together. With 2 knives or a pastry blender, cut in lard or shortening until pieces are the size of small peas. Mix egg yolk and water and stir into flour, salt, and fat mixture. Gather into a ball with your hands, flatten to 1 inch, and smooth edges. Dust with flour, wrap in plastic, and refrigerate until needed. Egg white will be used for glaze.

Food Processor Method: With steel blade in place, put flour, salt, and shortening into work bowl; process until there are no pieces larger than small peas. With machine running, add egg yolk and water mixed together, and process until dough forms a ball. Take out dough, dust with flour, smooth surface, wrap in plastic, and refrigerate until needed. Egg white will be used for glaze.

3. Meat Loaves, Meatballs, and Other Good Things With Ground Meat

MEAT LOAVES

Zucchini Meat Loaf

6 servings

Rice and zucchini make the beef go a long way in this loaf. It needs something creamy to accompany it—potatoes, celery, or mushrooms in a cream sauce, for instance, with some of the sauce served on the loaf slices. A green salad with cucumbers, and a little dill in the dressing, would be good with the loaf too.

For wine—a Rioja, Chianti, or California Zinfandel.

1 tablespoon butter
⅓ cup rice
2 tablespoons finely chopped
    onion
2 garlic cloves, minced
⅔ cup beef broth

½ pound zucchini, finely chopped
¼ cup fine, dry bread crumbs

1 pound lean ground beef
2 tablespoons chopped parsley
2 eggs
1 teaspoon salt
¼ teaspoon pepper
1 teaspoon oregano
2 slices bacon for top
  parsley or watercress for
    garnish

94

In a small saucepan with a lid, heat the butter and rice. Cook over low heat, stirring, until rice turns opaque and starts to brown. Add onion and garlic. Cook and stir until onion softens and becomes transparent, but not brown. Pour in broth, bring to a boil, stir once, cover, and simmer for 15 minutes, or until rice is tender and liquid has evaporated. Fluff with a fork and allow to cool slightly.

In a large bowl, combine zucchini and bread crumbs. Mix in beef, parsley, and rice. Lightly beat the eggs in a small bowl or measuring cup, and mix in salt, pepper, and oregano. Mix thoroughly with meat mixture.

Pack into oiled 9-by-5-by-3-inch loaf pan, doming the top slightly. Put the bacon slices on the loaf, and place in preheated 350°F oven for 1 hour.

Allow the loaf to stand 10–15 minutes before serving. With a spatula or egg turner, clear the sides of the loaf from the pan, move it from side to side and end to end of the pan to be sure it is free from the bottom. Turn out onto a warm platter, and serve surrounded by parsley or watercress.

Pork and Spinach Loaf   *4–6 servings*

Something creamy is good with this loaf—scalloped potatoes, or onions or mushrooms in a cream sauce, with some of the sauce served on the slices. Carrots, cooked or in salad form (recipes for both given), make an attractive second vegetable or salad. If the carrots are served hot, salad should be one without lettuce, since there is spinach in the loaf—sliced tomatoes, crisp raw or blanched vegetables, for instance. For dessert, slices of pound cake dribbled with Oloroso or Cream Sherry and topped with whipped cream would be easy and not too heavy.

Try a fruity, even lightly sweet wine with this—a Riesling or Sylvaner from Austria or Romania, Yugoslavia or Hungary, Washington or Chile, California or the Rhine. This wine, unlike a drier one, goes with dessert too.

1 pound ground pork
1 cup finely chopped celery
2 packages (10 ounces) frozen
    chopped spinach, thawed,
    drained, and squeezed dry
2 garlic cloves, minced
4–5 slices stale firm bread, crusts
    removed, torn into small
    pieces to make 2 cups
    crumbs
¼ cup heavy cream

1 egg
1¼ teaspoons salt
¼ teaspoon white pepper
½ teaspoon rosemary leaves,
    crumbled
⅛ teaspoon allspice
1 tablespoon cornstarch
2 hard-boiled eggs, chopped
2 slices bacon for top
    parsley or watercress for
    garnish

In a large mixing bowl, combine the ground pork, celery, well-squeezed spinach, and garlic. Scatter the crumbs on top, and pour the cream over them.

Beat the egg in a small bowl or measuring cup, and mix in the salt, pepper, rosemary and allspice. Add to the meat mixture and mix thoroughly. Add cornstarch and chopped eggs, and mix again.

Pack into a well-oiled 5-cup (8½-by-4½-by-2½-inch) loaf pan. Mound the top slightly, and spread bacon over the top. Place in a preheated 350°F oven and cook for 1¼ hours, or until loaf has shrunk away from the sides a bit, and a metal skewer pushed into the center comes out clean. Allow loaf to stand 15 minutes.

With a spatula or egg turner, clear the sides of the loaf from the pan, move it from side to side and end to end of the pan to be sure it is free from the bottom. Turn out onto a warm platter, and serve surrounded by parsley or watercress.

Five-Minute Carrots

4 cups coarsely shredded or
    julienned carrots
3 tablespoons water
4 tablespoons butter

½ teaspoon salt, or more to taste
¼ teaspoon freshly ground black
    pepper
¼ teaspoon ground ginger

Combine all ingredients in a heavy, lidded saucepan or casserole. Bring to a simmer, cover, and cook 5 minutes, or until tender.

Carrot Salad

Vegetables
4 cups grated carrots
½ green pepper, finely chopped

2 tablespoons minced shallots,
    or scallions with green tops

Dressing
5 teaspoons lemon juice
½ teaspoon Dijon mustard
1 tablespoon grated onion
¼ teaspoon salt

¼ teaspoon sugar
¼ cup salad oil
    freshly ground black pepper
    to taste

Combine vegetables. Mix together all dressing ingredients but oil and pepper. Beat in oil, add pepper, and mix with vegetables. Serve on a bed of Boston lettuce.

Balkan Meat Loaf

4–5 servings

Bulgur is the stretcher in this little loaf, its nutty taste and texture enhanced with Middle Eastern seasonings. It is topped with yogurt and fresh dill, and would be nice with green beans in tomato sauce (recipe given), and mashed potatoes. Hummus (recipe given)—that flavorful purée of garbanzo beans—with pita bread or sesame seed crackers would make an appropriate first course, and melons, in season, a refreshing dessert.

A cooled red wine, young and not too grand, perhaps with ice, some soda water, and a sliver of lemon, is good with this loaf. A jug wine, in short, or beer—or iced tea.

9–10-inch baking dish or cake pan

Bulgur
⅓ cup bulgur
⅔ cup boiling beef broth

⅛ teaspoon oregano
juice of ½ lemon

Put the bulgur in a small bowl and pour the boiling broth over it. Stir in the oregano, and soak for 1 hour, or until liquid is absorbed. Stir in lemon juice.

Meat Mixture

½ pound ground lean beef

½ pound ground lean lamb

1 egg ·

2 garlic cloves, chopped

1 teaspoon salt

⅛ teaspoon cayenne

2 teaspoons dried mint, crushed, or 2 tablespoons fresh mint, chopped

½ teaspoon ground coriander

1 teaspoon cumin

¼ cup beef broth

2 slices bacon

1 cup plain yogurt

¼ cup chopped fresh dill

Place the bulgur in a large bowl with the ground meat and mix well.

Beat the egg in a small bowl. Mash the garlic with the salt until there are no large pieces, and stir into the egg. Add the rest of the seasonings and the beef broth. Mix thoroughly with the meat and bulgur.

Form into a loaf about 8 inches long, cover with bacon strips, and place in an oiled baking dish. Cook in a preheated 350°F oven for 1 hour. Allow to stand for 10 minutes before serving. Mix half the dill with the yogurt, pour over the loaf, and serve sprinkled with the rest of the dill and surrounded by parsley sprigs.

Hummus

1 can (1 pound) garbanzo beans (chickpeas)

1 tablespoon finely chopped onion

2 garlic cloves, minced

1 teaspoon salt

⅛ teaspoon cayenne

½ cup vegetable oil or olive oil

1 tablespoon sesame oil (optional)

juice of 1 lemon (about ¼ cup)

chopped parsley and freshly ground pepper for garnish

Drain garbanzos in a sieve. Wash them by running cold water over them until water runs clear. Pat dry on paper towel.

Place garbanzos, onion, garlic, salt, and cayenne into the blender or food processor. Start the machine and add oil in a stream through the top or tube. Add lemon juice. Do not overblend or overprocess; it should have a little texture. Garnish with parsley and a few grinds of the pepper mill.

Green Beans in Tomato Sauce

1 pound fresh green beans
1 tablespoon olive oil
1 small onion, finely chopped
1 garlic clove, minced
½ teaspoon oregano

1 small bay leaf
2 cups (a 1-pound can) Italian
    tomatoes, chopped
salt and pepper to taste

If beans are small and tender, leave them whole. Cut large ones into 2-inch pieces. Cook in a large pot of well-salted water until bright green and just barely tender. Drain and rinse with cold water to prevent further cooking.

In a saucepan large enough to accommodate sauce and beans, heat the oil and cook onion and garlic until soft but not brown. Add oregano, bay leaf, and tomatoes. Cook for 20–25 minutes, or until sauce has lost its wateriness. Add salt and pepper to taste. Heat beans in the sauce.

Veal and Rice Loaf   *5–6 servings*

Ground veal—with cream, herbs, and a hint of lemon—has a seasoned rice-and-cheese mixture filling it like jelly in a jelly roll in this subtle little loaf. Serve it with something creamy: scalloped potatoes, or mushrooms in a cream sauce, and a green vegetable. The loaf could be preceded by soup or a cold first course, and followed by salad and a dessert rich in taste, light in texture—like a mousse.

Some might like young red wines with this, but whites are a possibility too—a sharp white like Portugal's Vinho Verde or a fuller white like California's Sauvignon Blanc or Italy's Pinot Grigio.

11-by-7-by-1½-inch baking dish

Filling
⅔ cup chicken broth
⅛ teaspoon savory
½ teaspoon butter

⅓ cup uncooked rice
½ cup Jarlsberg or Swiss cheese,
    coarsely grated

Bring broth to a boil. Add savory and butter, and stir in rice. Turn heat down, cover, and simmer for 15 minutes, or until liquid has been absorbed and rice is tender. Cool, stir in cheese, and set aside.

Meat Mixture

2–3 slices homemade-style bread,
  crusts removed, torn into
    1½ cups coarse crumbs
⅓ cup heavy cream
1 pound ground veal
1 egg
1 teaspoon salt

½ teaspoon freshly ground black
  pepper
½ teaspoon marjoram
¼ teaspoon savory
1 teaspoon minced zest of lemon
  (zest is rind with no white)
1 clove garlic, minced

Mix bread crumbs with cream and allow to stand for 10 minutes, then combine with veal. Beat the egg lightly and add the rest of the ingredients. Add egg mixture to meat mixture and mix well.

Assembly and Finish

2–3 slices bacon for top of loaf

¼ cup finely chopped parsley for
  garnish

On waxed paper, pat and press the meat mixture into a roughly 8-by-10-inch rectangle. Spread and pat rice and cheese on top, leaving an inch margin all around. With the help of the waxed paper, roll up like a jelly roll, starting with the narrow side. Press meat together to seal ends. Lift loaf in the waxed paper and ease onto an oiled baking dish, seam side down. Cover with bacon slices and place in preheated 400°F oven. Turn down at once to 350°F and bake for 45 minutes, or until no pink appears when loaf is pricked and pressed. Allow to stand 15 minutes before serving, sprinkled with parsley.

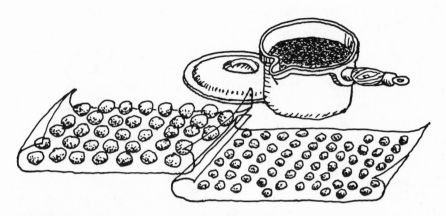

MEATBALLS AND SAUCES

Polpettine

6–8 servings

These are small meatballs, about the size of grapes. They cook quickly in a skillet, and are added to the sauce, needing no further cooking. Serve with any size of packaged spaghetti or linguine—1½ pounds of pasta for 6, 2 pounds for 8.

Meatballs (makes 64)
1 pound lean ground beef
2 tablespoons fine, dry bread
    crumbs (unseasoned)
¼ cup finely chopped parsley
1 teaspoon finely minced zest of
    lemon (zest is rind with no
    white)

1 egg
1 teaspoon salt
½ teaspoon pepper
1 teaspoon marjoram
¼ cup milk

For Browning
2 slices bacon

1 tablespoon butter

In a large mixing bowl, combine the beef, crumbs, parsley, and lemon rind. In a small bowl, beat the egg lightly, and add the seasonings and milk. Stir to mix, then mix thoroughly with meat mixture.

Form meat mixture into 64 balls, ¾-inch in diameter, by rolling lightly in the palms of the hands.

In a large, heavy 11-inch skillet, cook the bacon until crisp. Place it on paper towel to drain. Add butter to the fat in the pan, and when the foam subsides, put in half the meatballs. Cook on moderately high heat, shaking the pan constantly, until balls have lost their red color and are brown here and there. With a slotted spoon, transfer the balls as they are done to the sauce. Do the rest of the balls the same way. They will all be done in 2–3 minutes.

Stir the balls into the sauce carefully, bring to a simmer, and cook 5 minutes for flavors to combine. Crumble the bacon on top. Serve on individual portions of pasta. Offer freshly grated Parmesan in a small bowl.

Tomato Sauce (makes 6 cups)

2 tablespoons olive oil	1 teaspoon salt
1 medium onion, finely chopped (1 cup)	½ teaspoon pepper
	¼ cup chopped fresh basil, or 2 teaspoons dried basil
2 garlic cloves, minced	
2 cans (1 pound, 13 ounces) Italian tomatoes, put through food mill or whirled in food processor	1 bay leaf
	¼ teaspoon crushed red-pepper flakes, or more to taste

In a heavy, lidded saucepan, preferably enameled ironware, heat the oil, add the onions and garlic, and cook over low heat until onions are soft and transparent but not brown. If food processor is used for tomatoes, do not overprocess—whirl only until all large pieces are broken up. Add the tomatoes and seasonings to the onions and garlic. Bring to a boil, turn down heat, and simmer, partially covered, for 25 minutes.

Koenigsberger Klopse   6 servings of 5 meatballs each

Anchovy haters will never know anchovies are the magic ingredient in these German meatballs. Caper haters you can't fool because capers are evident in the sauce, but you might make converts.

Serve the klopse (meatballs) with boiled potatoes or noodles. Hot buttered beets, black bread, a green salad, and a wicked strudel could complete the meal.

A German wine that says Kabinett on the label will not be as sweet as some, and might be good with the klopse, or, of course, beer.

Flameproof lidded casserole or pan, about 11 inches in diameter.

Meatballs

1 pound ground beef (or ½ pound beef, ½ pound pork)
¼ cup finely chopped fresh parsley
3 tablespoons finely chopped scallions
  grated rind of ½ lemon
4 anchovy fillets, chopped

2 slices stale homemade-style bread, crusts removed
½ cup heavy cream
1 egg
½ teaspoon salt
¼ teaspoon pepper
⅛ teaspoon nutmeg

Put the meat, parsley, scallions, lemon rind, and anchovy fillets into a large mixing bowl. Crumble the bread, or tear it, to make about 1 cup of crumbs. Scatter them on top of the contents of the mixing bowl. Pour the cream over, moistening all the crumbs. Stir to mix. In a small bowl or measuring cup, beat the egg lightly, and add the salt, pepper, and nutmeg. Add to the meat mixture and mix well, until mixture is dry enough to be shaped into balls. Form into 30 balls. They are now to be cooked in the sauce, without browning.

Sauce

4 tablespoons butter
4 tablespoons flour
1 can (13¾ ounces) beef broth
¾ cup beer

1 teaspoon brown sugar
¼ cup drained capers

fresh dill or parsley for garnish

Melt butter in a saucepan and stir in flour to make a smooth paste. Remove from heat and add broth and beer gradually, stirring until there are no lumps. Put back on the heat and cook, stirring, until mixture thickens. Add sugar (to counteract any bitterness from the beer), and capers.

Place the meatballs in a lidded flameproof casserole or pan large enough to take the meatballs in one layer. Pour the sauce over them, make sure none are stuck to the bottom, cover, and cook for 30 minutes, stirring occasionally. Skim off fat, and serve sprinkled with chopped fresh dill or parsley.

Ham Balls   *6 servings of 6 meatballs each*

Although these meatballs can make a very presentable main course out of that leftover ham, they are good enough to warrant going out and buying a pound of ham to grind yourself in meat grinder or food processor.

Serve with buttered thin noodles. A green vegetable and a salad of oranges, cucumbers, and scallions (recipe given) would look and taste right with that combination. Crusty bread, a cheese tray, and fruit could follow.

A cool white wine—Chardonnay or an Italian dry white—could make the meal an occasion.

Note: *Fresh dill is essential for this dish.*

Ham Balls

1 pound ground cooked ham
   (2½–3 cups)
¼ cup minced scallions (use
   some crisp green tops)
½ cup fine, dry bread crumbs,
   unseasoned
2 teaspoons finely chopped fresh
   dill

¼ teaspoon white pepper
1 teaspoon Dijon mustard
1 egg

1 tablespoon butter, more if
   needed
1 tablespoon oil, more if needed

Mix all ingredients together, except butter and oil. Form into 36 one-inch balls. Heat butter and oil in a large, heavy skillet. When butter stops foaming, lightly brown the balls in batches. Keep warm in a serving dish while sauce is being made.

Sauce

1 cup sour cream (8 ounces)
2 tablespoons flour
1 cup water
¼ teaspoon white pepper

½ teaspoon salt, or to taste
3 tablespoons finely chopped
   fresh dill

Stir sour cream and flour together in a saucepan. Gradually stir in water and cook on low flame, stirring constantly, until bubbling and thickened. Add pepper, salt, and dill. Pour over ham balls, sprinkled with a little finely chopped fresh dill, or decorated with long sprigs.

Orange and Cucumber Salad

4 small navel oranges, peeled (leaving no white) and thinly sliced

1 medium cucumber, scrubbed, trimmed, scored with a fork and thinly sliced

¼ cup finely chopped scallions

1 small head Boston lettuce, washed, dried, and broken up

½ cup French dressing

French Dressing

¼ teaspoon salt, or more to taste

⅛ teaspoon freshly ground black pepper

½ teaspoon Dijon mustard

2 tablespoons cider or wine vinegar

6 tablespoons olive oil, salad oil, or a mixture

Mix salt, pepper, and mustard with the vinegar. Beat in the oil and taste, adding more salt if desired.

Arrange salad ingredients in bowl and toss with dressing just before serving.

Yogurt Khoreshe

6 servings

Khoreshe means stew in the Middle East. This one comes from the eastern end, closer to India, where curry, turmeric, and raisins in the rice appear along with the prevailing lamb and yogurt.

The lamb is in the form of meatballs, and they cook in chicken broth seasoned with curry, cardamom, and cloves. The yogurt goes in at the end. With its accompanying rice (recipe given), bright with turmeric and accented with raisins, the khoreshe is a pleasantly exotic affair.

Pecans toasted in butter would be nice with drinks before the meal; hot pita bread, chutney, and a fresh, crisp salad of cucumbers and scallions would be just the thing with the khoreshe; and for dessert, lime sherbet and some elegant, lacy cookies. All you need then is a pomegranate for the final Middle Eastern touch.

Wine doesn't go too well with a spicy dish like this. Beer or tea would be better.

1 pound lean ground lamb
2–3 slices stale homemade-style
   bread, crusts removed
¾ teaspoon salt
¼ teaspoon pepper
1 teaspoon turmeric
¼–½ cup cold water
2 tablespoons oil
1 medium onion, finely chopped

2 teaspoons flour
4–6 whole cloves, broken up
2 teaspoons curry powder
1 teaspoon ground cardamom
1 cup chicken broth

1 cup yogurt
   fresh mint leaves, coarsely
    chopped, or chopped parsley

Put meat into a large mixing bowl. Tear bread into small bits, or crumble to make about 1½ cups of crumbs. Strew over meat. Sprinkle salt, pepper, and turmeric over crumbs, and pour on ¼ cup water. Stir and toss with fork or fingers to mix well. Add a little more water if needed to make mixture soft and light, capable of sticking together in balls. With clean, wet hands, make into 24 balls, about 1 inch in diameter.

In a large heavy skillet, heat oil until a haze appears over it. Brown meatballs, a few at a time, turning and shaking them in the pan. As they brown, transfer them with a slotted spoon to a lidded casserole that will take them in one layer. Pour off all but a thin film of oil from skillet and put in onions. Cook for a minute or two and add to the meatballs in the casserole. Sprinkle flour, cloves, curry and cardamom over onions and meat, and stir carefully over low heat for 1 minute. Pour in broth, bring to a boil, then turn down heat. Cover and simmer for 35 minutes, shaking casserole from time to time to keep meatballs from sticking. Tip casserole and skim off fat.

Cool ¼ cup of the sauce slightly, and beat it into yogurt. Pour mixture into casserole and heat but do not boil.

Serve surrounded by—or along with—Lemon Rice, sprinkled if possible with fresh mint, otherwise sprinkled with parsley.

Lemon Rice

3 tablespoons butter
2 tablespoons oil
1½ teaspoons mustard seeds
1 tablespoon turmeric
1½ teaspoons salt
4½ cups cooked rice (1½ cups raw
    rice cooked in 3 cups water,
    1 tablespoon butter, and *no*
    salt)

juice of 1 large lemon
⅓ cup raisins, soaked in boiling
    water for 10 minutes

In a lidded 2–2½-quart saucepan, heat the butter and add the mustard seeds, turmeric, and salt. Stir and cook on low heat until the mustard seeds jump. Add the rice and stir until all is blended and heated through. Add the lemon juice and drained raisins, and mix again.

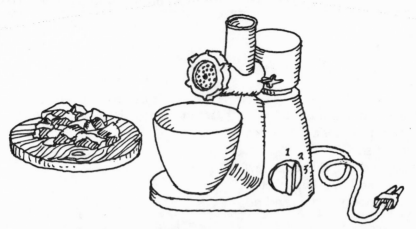

...AND OTHER GOOD THINGS WITH GROUND MEAT

Chilean Corn Pie

6–8 servings

This is quite a concoction, and if it ever was really Chilean, it has probably changed a lot as the recipe has been handed from friend to friend. You can make your own changes, controlling the hotness and the quantities of corn and beans. For a spectacular presentation, which unfortunately does not last long, try the soufflé version of the topping given at the end of the recipe. Just be sure the container is deep enough to take the puffed soufflé effect while it lasts.

Corn chips, some Cheddar cheese, and strips of roasted or raw green and red peppers would be a good starter for the meal, and then all you need is a big green salad and crusty bread. They like coconut in Chile—perhaps some coconut cookies with ice cream would be an appropriate dessert.

Margaritas, tequila on the rocks, or rum drinks could precede the meal, and beer or a Chilean red wine could go along with it.

2½-quart baking dish (9 by 13 by 2 inches, approximately), or 3-quart soufflé dish

2 tablespoons oil
1 medium onion, finely chopped
1 green pepper, coarsely chopped
2 garlic cloves, minced
1 pound lean ground beef
1 teaspoon salt
2 tablespoons chili powder
8 ounces (1 cup) canned or frozen green chilies, drained and chopped
1 can (1 pound) Italian tomatoes, chopped

2 cups cooked corn niblets, off the cob, frozen or canned, drained (reserve 1 cup for topping)
1 can (1 pound) red kidney beans, drained, juice reserved
½ cup raisins, soaked in hot water for 10 minutes
1 cup sliced pitted black olives

Heat the oil in a large, heavy skillet, or wide flameproof casserole that can be covered, and cook the onion, green pepper, and garlic until onion is limp but not brown. Crumble in meat and cook, stirring and breaking up lumps, until beef loses its pink color. Add salt, chili powder, chilies, and tomatoes. Bring to a boil, cover, and simmer for 20 minutes. Stir in corn, beans, raisins, and olives. Cover and simmer another 10–15 minutes. Taste and add salt if needed.

The degree of wetness is up to you. If mixture seems too wet, cook it that last few minutes without a lid, longer if needed to dry it more. If it seems too dry, moisten with reserved bean liquid and/or a little hot water, and simmer covered as directed. When done, turn into a baking dish or soufflé dish.

Topping

1½ cups milk
¾ teaspoon salt
½ cup cornmeal
1 cup sharp Cheddar cheese

1 cup cooked corn kernels (reserved from above 2 cups)
3 eggs

Bring milk to a boil, with the salt. Gradually add the cornmeal, stirring constantly, and cook until mixture thickens. Add cheese, stirring until cheese melts. Remove from heat, allow to cool slightly, and stir in eggs, lightly beaten. For this version, use 2½-quart baking dish for meat mixture and pour topping over it. Bake in preheated 350°F oven for 20–30 minutes, until lightly browned.

For soufflé version, put meat mixture into 3-quart wide, shallow casserole, or 3-quart soufflé dish. Separate eggs, and mix lightly beaten yolks with slightly cooled, cooked milk, salt, and cornmeal. Beat whites until stiff and fold into topping mixture. Spread over meat mixture and bake as above.

Ed Romero's Red Chili Enchiladas   *6 servings*

When I asked my Sante Fe friend Ed Romero about the origin of his Red Chile Enchilada recipe, he said it was pure Indian, Spanish, Mexican, and Southwest USA. Since the essential ingredient is a particular kind of chili, that seemingly imprecise background may in fact pinpoint the recipe in New Mexico, famous for its variety of chilies, and to Sante Fe in particular, where chilies are used to such good advantage.

When tomatoes are at their best and fresh basil is available, leave out the tomatoes served with the enchiladas and have a big tomato and basil salad. An accompanying vegetable dish dear to Santa Feans is calabacitas, a combination of corn, squash, and garlic (recipe given). Whether or not to put in hot chilies is a subject for fierce arguments, pro and con. The recipe given here is a pro. Feel free to leave them out if you are con.

Margaritas, corn chips, and crisp vegetables with a dip could start the meal, and a Spanish or Mexican flan—or fruit—could end it. Beer is best to drink with the enchiladas.

By the way, Ed says to save the chili seeds for the chickens; they encourage them to lay in the winter.

2 heavy skillets: one 7–8 inches for cooking tortillas, one 10–11 inches for the meat and chili mixture; 6 ovenproof dinner plates

12–15 dried mild red chilies, 3–6 inches long
1 rounded tablespoon lard
1 medium onion, coarsely chopped
3 garlic cloves (good size), minced

1 pound coarsely ground lean pork
2 tablespoons flour
¾ teaspoon ground cumin seeds
1 teaspoon oregano
2 teaspoons salt
1 tablespoon vinegar

To Serve:

1–2 tablespoons lard, enough to be ¼-inch deep melted in 7–8-inch skillet

12 soft, white corn tortillas

1 large Spanish onion, coarsely chopped

3 cans pinto or red kidney beans

4 fresh tomatoes, in 8 wedges each

2 cups chopped crisp lettuce

1½ cups grated Cheddar cheese

Break stems off chilies and remove seeds. Put chilies in hot water to cover, and allow them to soak for 15 minutes. This cleans the outside and softens the flesh somewhat. Drain chilies and place in blender. Add 1 cup water and blend briefly. Keep blending and adding water, a little at a time, until you have about 5 cups of smooth liquid a little thinner than cream. Leave in blender while you prepare pork.

Melt and heat lard in a large, heavy skillet. Put in onions and garlic, and cook until onions are limp but not brown. Crumble in ground pork and cook, stirring, over medium heat until pieces are of uniform size and no pink shows. Remove from heat and sprinkle in flour, stirring until no white shows. With skillet still off heat, pour puréed chilies from the blender through a strainer into pork mixture. Straining removes skin and seeds that would add a bitter or too-hot taste.

Put skillet back on heat, add cumin, oregano, and salt, and stir to mix well. Bring to a simmer, stir in vinegar, and simmer for about 20 minutes, stirring frequently. If mixture thickens too much, add a little hot water. Mixture is to be poured over tortillas, so it should not be too dry, but not watery either. If it is too watery, cook slightly longer. Check seasoning.

To Serve

It helps to have two people for the final assembly: one to cook the tortillas, the other to put everything together on the plates.

In a saucepan, heat the beans in their liquid. Have ready: 6 dinner plates, 12 tortillas, chopped Spanish onion, tomato wedges, chopped lettuce, and grated cheese. Heat lard in smaller skillet, and when it is just short of smoking, put in a tortilla and cook until barely soft and pliable, before it becomes crisp, turning once. Lift from the small skillet to the large one, turn once to coat with sauce, and then place flat on a dinner plate. This is where a helper is needed. Spoon some of the chili and meat mixture over the tortilla, then some beans, then some chopped onion. Cover with another cooked tortilla, repeat the addition of sauce, beans, and onion, and this time sprinkle cheese on top. Do all the plates the same way, and place them in preheated 350°F oven for 3–5 minutes, or until cheese is melted.

Surround each enchilada with chopped lettuce and tomato wedges, and serve.

Calabacitas

2 tablespoons lard
3 medium zucchini, coarsely
    chopped (about 1½ pounds)
1 medium onion, coarsely
    chopped (about 1 cup)
1 garlic clove, minced

2 packages (10 ounces each)
    frozen corn niblets
1 can (4 ounces) peeled green
    chilies (not jalapeño),
    chopped
salt to taste

In a large, heavy skillet or shallow casserole with a lid, melt the lard and cook the onions and garlic until the onions are transparent. Add zucchini and cook for a minute or two, stirring frequently. Add corn and green chilies. Cover and cook until corn is done, about 5 minutes. Turn into warm serving dish.

Piñon   *6 servings*

Practically the national dish of Puerto Rico, this recipe comes from Carlos Esteva of Ron Rico Rum, whose version is famous. Serve with rice and chickpeas, accompanied by a large green salad that includes tomatoes. Start off with rum drinks, the favorite on the island being rum and water, with or without a wedge of lime or lemon. Beer is best with piñon. Dessert might be rum cake or fresh fruit.

Note: *When plantains cannot be found, a good version can be made by substituting slices of yam, cut ¼-inch thick.*

Bake in 2–2½ quart baking dish or casserole

5 ripe plantains
½ cup (1 stick) butter or margarine
1 large onion, chopped
1 large garlic clove, minced
½ green pepper, seeded,
    deribbed, and chopped
½ teaspoon oregano
1 pound lean ground beef
1 tablespoon capers

6 tablespoons canned tomato
    sauce
½ pound french-cut green beans,
    cooked, or 1 package
    (10 ounces) frozen french-
    cut green beans, cooked
salt and pepper
3 eggs

Peel plantains and slice them each lengthwise four times. Place cut plantains in 1 quart water with 1 tablespoon salt until needed.

Heat 2 tablespoons of the butter or margarine in a large, heavy skillet, and put in the onion, garlic, green pepper, and oregano. Stir and cook for a minute or two. Crumble in the ground meat, cook, and stir, breaking up the lumps, until meat has lost its color. Stir in capers and tomato sauce, and add salt and pepper to taste. Cook uncovered for 15 minutes, stirring occasionally.

Mix in the beans and check seasoning.

Remove plantains from the salt water and dry them. In another skillet, using the rest of the butter or margarine, fry the plantain slices, turning them over until they are golden brown. Set them aside on a plate.

Butter a large baking dish and, starting with plantains, make alternate layers of plantains and the meat mixture, ending with plantains.

Beat the eggs until they are fluffy, pour over the top layer, and place in a preheated 325°F oven for 25–30 minutes, or until heated through.

Russian Beef Patties

6 servings

These hearty little patties, with their touch of caraway, make a handsome sight under a coating of sour cream mixed with tomato sauce. Buttered beets and skillet cucumbers (recipe given) would be good with them, for color and taste. Poppy seed noodles could supply the starchy accompaniment. For this, simply stir a tablespoon or two of poppy seeds and a little more butter into the noodles.

A cooled red wine like Beaujolais, or one of the Loires like Chinon, or beer could be served, but for an exceptional taste combination, sip chilled vodka.

for 2½-quart baking dish (9 by 13 by 2 inches, approximately)

1 pound lean ground beef	½ teaspoon freshly ground black
5 slices homemade-style bread,	pepper
crusts removed	½ teaspoon caraway seeds
½ cup milk	¼–½ cup cold water
1 small onion, finely chopped	2 tablespoons oil
(about ½ cup)	2 tablespoons butter
2 tablespoons finely chopped	
parsley	1 cup sour cream
1 teaspoon salt	½ cup canned tomato sauce
	sprinkle of paprika

Put ground beef into a large bowl. Tear bread into crumbs and add to the bowl with milk, onion, parsley, salt, pepper, and caraway seeds. Mix lightly and add water, a small amount at a time, beating until mixture is fluffy. Form into 12 patties that will fit into your baking dish comfortably. If possible, refrigerate for a while.

Heat butter and oil in a heavy skillet and brown patties on both sides. Do them in batches, blot on paper towel, and place in baking dish. Mix together sour cream and tomato sauce. Place in preheated 350°F oven for 6–8 minutes. Cooking too long makes the sour cream curdle, so leave in the oven just long enough to heat sour-cream mixture. Serve sprinkled with paprika.

Skillet Cucumbers

The cucumbers are not fried, they are cooked in butter and their own juice until tender-crisp and still white.

3 cucumbers, 8 inches long   salt and pepper
2 tablespoons butter   ¼ cup finely chopped parsley

Trim off ends of cucumbers, peel, and cut in half lengthwise. Remove seeds with a spoon, and cut halves across in ⅜-inch slices. Melt butter in a large skillet and stir in cucumbers. Turn down heat and cook cucumbers, stirring and sprinkling with salt and pepper, until they are tender and hot, but not soft. Stir in parsley.

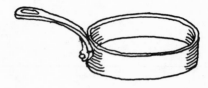

4. A Quartet of Old Favorites... Deliciously Stretched

Moussaka

8–10 *servings*

One of the best known Middle Eastern dishes, moussaka is splendid party fare. This Greek version is made of layers of eggplant and well-seasoned meat, liberally laced with Parmesan, topped with a rich, creamy white sauce and brought to a golden brown in the oven.

Lamb is often used instead of beef, but it is easier to find lean ground beef than lamb. If you have a food processor or meat grinder, and want to use lamb, buy a little more than a pound of shoulder lamb, trim off most of the fat (some is needed for juiciness) and grind it yourself.

Rice and green beans are logical accompaniments, with a salad of thinly sliced tomatoes, red onions, and green peppers. Lemon instead of vinegar in its dressing and a sprinkle of oregano will give a Greek touch to the salad.

Pita bread, now widely available, would be a nice change from French or Italian. Try cutting them in four pieces, buttering the inside, sprinkling lightly with oregano, and heating in the oven.

To carry through the theme, the meal could begin with avgo lemono soup and end with store-bought baklava or, if calories count, a big fruit salad.

The pine-pitch taste of Retsina is traditional, but some people don't like it. The safest choice is dry white wine (Soave), or a soft, young red (Bardolino, Valpolicella) from Italy.

118

14-by-10-by-2-inch baking pan

Eggplant

4 medium eggplants
2 tablespoons oil

2 tablespoons butter
salt and pepper

Wash the eggplants, trim off the ends, and cut in ½-inch slices. Do not peel. In a large, heavy skillet, heat the oil and butter, and cook the slices quickly, a few at a time, until they are just touched with brown. Don't let them stay in the pan too long—they soak up the fat. Remove cooked slices to drain on paper towels. Make several layers, with a base of newspaper. Sprinkle with salt and pepper as they cook. Use more oil and butter if needed. Set aside.

Meat Layer

2 tablespoons oil
3 medium onions, finely chopped
1 garlic clove, minced
1 pound lean ground beef
1 can (1 pound) Italian tomatoes,
    drained and coarsely
    chopped (save juice)

½ cup dry red wine
¼ cup finely chopped parsley
1¼ teaspoons salt
¼ teaspoon freshly ground black
    pepper
½ teaspoon each cinnamon and
    oregano

Heat the oil in a large, heavy skillet, and cook the onions and garlic over low heat until the onions are soft but not brown. Crumble in the meat and cook over higher heat, stirring and breaking up lumps, until meat is beginning to brown. Stir in the tomatoes, wine, parsley, and seasonings. Bring to a boil, turn down to a simmer, and cook 15–20 minutes, or until mixture is almost dry. Set aside, and pour off any fat that appears as the mixture cools. If mixture gets too dry, add reserved juice from tomatoes.

Sauce

¼ pound (1 stick) butter
½ cup flour
 4 cups milk (1 quart)
1½ teaspoons salt

¼ teaspoon white pepper
⅛ teaspoon nutmeg
5 eggs
2 cups cottage cheese

Melt butter in a 2½-quart saucepan, and stir in flour to make a smooth paste. Off the heat, add milk, and whisk until there are no lumps. Stir in salt, pepper, and nutmeg, and cook, stirring constantly, until sauce is thick and smooth. Remove from heat and allow to cool, stirring occasionally to keep skin from forming. When sauce is cool, stir in well-beaten eggs, and cottage cheese.

Assembly

1 cup fine, dry unseasoned bread crumbs	1 cup freshly grated Parmesan cheese

Lightly grease a baking pan and sprinkle with 3–4 tablespoons of crumbs. Mix the rest of the crumbs with the Parmesan cheese.

Make 3 layers in the pan: eggplant on the bottom, meat mixture in the middle, and eggplant on the top. Sprinkle each layer with ¼ of the crumbs-and-cheese mixture.

Pour the sauce over the top layer of eggplant, and sprinkle with the remaining ¼ of the crumbs-and-cheese mixture. Place in a preheated 350°F oven and bake for 50–60 minutes, or until puffed and golden. Allow the moussaka to stand for 15–20 minutes before serving. Cut down the middle the long way, and across to make 8 or 10 portions.

Pastitsio   *8–10 servings*

To describe pastitsio as a layer of meat between layers of macaroni and cheese, although accurate, is to do the dish a great injustice. The meat is delectably seasoned with herbs and spices, the sauce that permeates the whole thing is a creamy marvel of white sauce and eggs, and the cheese is Parmesan. In northern Greece, where the dish originated, it is served as a Sunday or holiday treat.

Zucchini in a simple tomato sauce makes a good companion for the pastitsio, with a salad of greens to follow. Dessert could be sliced oranges with a little sugar and a few drops of kirsch.

There are some soft and fruity red wines from Greece, but if you can't find one, try a Nebbiolo or Spanna from northern Italy, or Zinfandel from California.

3-quart baking dish, 14 by 10 by 2 inches, approximately

Meat Layer

2 tablespoons butter
3 medium onions, finely chopped
1 garlic clove, minced
1 pound lean ground beef
1 can (1 pound) Italian tomatoes, drained, chopped, juice reserved

¾ cup dry red wine
1¼ teaspoons salt
½ teaspoon freshly ground black pepper
½ teaspoon each cinnamon, nutmeg, oregano

In a large, heavy skillet, heat the butter and cook the onions and garlic over low heat until the onions are limp and transparent but not brown. Crumble in the meat, and cook over slightly higher heat, stirring and breaking up lumps, until the meat has lost its pink and is beginning to brown.

Add tomatoes, wine, and seasonings. After mixture comes to a boil, turn down to a simmer, and cook over low heat for 15–20 minutes, or until most of the liquid has evaporated. Allow to cool, and remove fat as it appears.

Macaroni and Sauce

12 ounces elbow macaroni
1 teaspoon oil
6 tablespoons butter
6 tablespoons flour

4 cups milk (1 quart)
1 teaspoon salt
¼ teaspoon white pepper

In 6–8 quarts boiling salted water, with oil added to prevent sticking, cook the macaroni until it loses its starchy taste, but is still slightly firm to the teeth (al dente). Drain and set aside.

In a saucepan, melt the butter and add the flour. Stir over very low heat until smooth. Remove from the heat, add the milk, salt, and pepper, and stir until there are no lumps. Cook over low heat, stirring, until sauce is thick and creamy. Set aside to cool. Stir occasionally to keep a crust from forming.

Assembly

4 eggs, beaten
¾ cup unseasoned fine, dry bread crumbs

1¼ cups freshly grated Parmesan cheese
1–2 tablespoons butter for top and baking dish

Whisk ½ cup of cooled sauce into well-beaten eggs, then add mixture to the rest of the sauce. Stir in ¼ cup of the Parmesan cheese.

Butter the baking pan, and sprinkle with ¼ cup of the bread crumbs. Spread ½ the macaroni in the pan over the crumbs. Sprinkle with ¼ cup Parmesan.

Stir ¼ cup of crumbs and ¼ cup of Parmesan into the meat mixture. If this dries the mixture, add reserved juice from the tomatoes. Spread the meat evenly over the macaroni, and cover with half the sauce. Sprinkle with ¼ cup Parmesan.

Spread the rest of the macaroni over the sauced meat, cover with the rest of the sauce, and sprinkle with remaining crumbs and Parmesan cheese mixed together. Dot with butter.

Place baking dish in preheated 350°F oven for 40–50 minutes, or until top is golden brown and puffed. Allow to stand for 15 minutes before cutting into 8 or 10 portions.

Kate Tremper's Lasagne   *20 or more servings*

This is one of my daughter Kate's triumphs. She has served it with great success many times, and nobody has ever missed the extra pound or more of meat that usually goes into an expanded lasagna recipe. She also suggests something different in the way of salad, which can almost obviate the need for dessert.

The salad is made of peeled oranges, sliced or cut up, with pitted black olives and scallions, in a vinaigrette made with lemon instead of vinegar, served on lettuce leaves.

The lasagne recipe looks long, but it is broken up into steps, and there is nothing difficult about it.

18-by-13-by-2½-inch roasting pan

1 pound lasagne noodles, cooked according to package directions and set to drain

Tomato Sauce

4 cans (1 pound, 3 ounces each) Italian tomatoes, chopped

1 can (6 ounces) tomato paste

2 cans (8 ounces each) tomato sauce

1 teaspoon salt

1 bay leaf

2 cloves garlic, minced

2 medium onions, chopped

1 teaspoon oregano

½ teaspoon thyme

½ teaspoon marjoram

Mix all ingredients, cover, and cook on low heat for about 1½ hours. Sauce is done when it has come together into a pleasant thickness, without the wateriness it starts out with. Keep checking after 1 hour.

Meat Mixture

1 tablespoon olice oil

1 small onion, chopped (½ cup)

1 garlic clove, minced

1 pound lean ground beef

¼ teaspoon oregano

½ teaspoon salt

¼ teaspoon pepper

Heat oil in a large skillet. Cook onions and garlic until onions are transparent. Crumble in ground beef and cook over fairly high heat, stirring and breaking up lumps, until no pink shows. Stir in oregano and salt. Pour off any excessive fat.

Zucchini

1½ pounds zucchini, washed, trimmed, in ¼-inch slices

Cheese Mixture

2 pounds ricotta or cottage cheese

1 cup freshly grated Parmesan cheese (¼ pound)

2 eggs, lightly beaten

¼ teaspoon pepper

½ teaspoon salt, if needed

½ pound full-fat Mozzarella or Muenster cheese, in thin slices for top

Mix together ricotta or cottage cheese, ½ cup of the Parmesan, eggs, and pepper. Taste and add salt unless cheeses supply enough. Reserve Mozzarella or Muenster until final assembly.

Assembly

1. Spread a thin layer of sauce on the bottom of roasting pan.
2. Cover sauce with a layer of noodles.
3. Spread with a little sauce and all the meat mixture. Spread ½ the zucchini on top of meat, with a little sauce on top.
4. Place another layer of noodles over sauced zucchini.
5. Spread with some sauce, the cheese mixture, the rest of the zucchini, and some sauce.
6. Lay the rest of the noodles on top, the rest of the sauce, the Mozzarella or Muenster slices, and sprinkle with remaining ½ cup of Parmesan.

Place in preheated 350°F oven and bake for 45 minutes—covered with foil for 30 minutes, uncovered for 15. If cheese on top has not melted and browned lightly, put under broiler for a minute or two.

Spanish Rice, New Mexico Style   *6–8 servings*

Lime juice and hot peppers are refreshing accents for this ancient and usually bland dish. The rice is cooked in a tomato sauce, and the meat, cooked separately, lies on top. With a squeeze of lime and a garnish of lime wedges and olives, it is good-looking and certainly not bland.

Serve guacamole (avocado purée, recipe given) with taco or corn chips, and a big fancy salad, full of crisp vegetables and assorted greens. Dessert could be rich and fattening after such a simple main course—layer cake and ice cream, or lemon meringue pie.

Red wine with orange, lemon, lime, and a little sugar (your own Sangria) would be good with this; or white wine and soda, with lime slices and ice; or beer.

Sauce

2 tablespoons olive oil
1 medium onion, chopped
    (about 1 cup)
2 garlic cloves, minced
1 can (35 ounces) Italian
    tomatoes (or 2 one-pound
    cans)

1½ jalapeño peppers, minced, or
    1 canned green chili,
    chopped (this is variable
    to taste)
1 tablespoon oregano
1 teaspoon ground cumin
    salt to taste

Heat the oil and cook onion and garlic until onion is limp. Add tomatoes, hot pepper, oregano, cumin, and salt to taste. Cook for 20 minutes. Makes 4 cups—3 for rice, 1 for meat.

Rice

2 tablespoons olive oil	1½ teaspoons salt
2 cloves garlic, peeled	½ teaspoon pepper
2 cups rice	1 cup sliced olives—½ pitted
1 cup water	black and ½ stuffed green
3 cups sauce (above)	

Heat the oil in a lidded saucepan and cook the garlic cloves until they almost brown, then discard them. Add the rice, cook and stir over low heat until rice becomes opaque, then golden. Add water, sauce, salt, pepper, and olives. Bring to a boil, stir once, cover and cook over low heat for 20 minutes, or until rice is tender and liquid has been absorbed.

Meat

1 tablespoon olive oil	1 teaspoon oregano
1 small onion, chopped (½ cup)	½ teaspoon ground cumin
1 pound lean ground beef	salt and pepper

Heat oil in a large, heavy skillet. Cook onion until it is soft but not brown. Crumble in the meat, sprinkle with oregano, cumin, salt, and pepper. Cook until meat loses its color and begins to brown, stirring constantly to break up lumps. Add the last cup of sauce, and cook for 15–20 minutes, until most of the liquid has cooked away. Mixture should be moist but not too wet. Skim off any obvious fat, and taste to check salt and pepper.

Finish

juice of 1 lime	putted black olives and
lime wedges	stuffed green olives

Arrange rice on a hot platter or serving dish. Spread the meat mixture on top and squeeze the lime juice over all. Garnish with lime wedges and sliced olives.

Guacamole

2 medium-size ripe avocados
1 tablespoon lemon juice
2 tablespoons grated onion
1 small garlic clove, chopped
¼ teaspoon salt

few drops of Tabasco, or 2
   tablespoons chopped
   canned green chilies
1 medium-size firm tomato,
   peeled, seeded, and chopped
freshly ground pepper to taste

Halve the avocados lengthwise and remove stones; spoon flesh into a small bowl and mash with lemon juice and onion. On a saucer, mash garlic with salt until no large pieces remain. Add with rest of ingredients to the avocado mixture. Place a piece of plastic wrap directly on surface and chill for 1–2 hours.

5. The Crêpe Approach

Main-Course Crêpes

These thin, elegant French pancakes can be used with great success to make main courses without much meat. Folded over a filling of meat and vegetables, they can be lined up in a baking dish, buttered or sauced and heated for serving.

Crêpes call for wines easy to drink—those you prefer to swallow rather than sip—and a chilled rosé or white from a jug is fine. Cider is often drunk with crêpes in Brittany; beer is good.

Crêpes   *about 16 crêpes, 6½ inches in diameter*

½ cup water   2 cups sifted flour
1½ cups milk   4 tablespoons melted butter
 4 eggs   oil for the pan
½ teaspoon salt

Put the ingredients, except oil for the pan, into a blender in the order listed. Cover and blend for about 1 minute, or until smooth. Pour into a 4-cup measuring cup. Using a wadded paper towel or a brush, oil the bottom and sides of a 6½-inch skillet or crêpe pan. Place the pan over moderate heat until it is just beginning to smoke. With the left hand, pour about ¼ cup of batter into the pan, removing from the heat immediately with the right hand. Quickly swirl the batter around the pan to coat the bottom, and pour out excess into a small bowl. (The batter left on the side of the pan from pouring out will serve as a little handle with which to turn the crêpe.) Put the pan back on the heat and almost immediately start loosening the edges of the crêpe with a spatula, including the little handle. Shake the pan to keep the crêpe loose from the bottom. Lift an edge with the spatula, and when crêpe is lightly brown it is done on that side. All this takes about 1 minute.

Using the handle, turn the crêpe onto its other side, and cook a few seconds, until it is spotted with brown. Remove to a plate. Continue, greasing the pan each time, until you have 16 good ones piled up. Batter poured off into the small bowl may be used, of course, but may need to be strained.

Crêpes may be frozen, well wrapped in plastic or foil. Allow to come to room temperature before trying to use.

Ham and Spinach Crêpes
Chicken and Spinach Crêpes

8 servings of
2 crêpes each

The same basic recipe fills these crêpes, with a slight adjustment of seasonings when chicken is used instead of ham. Stracciatelli (recipe given) is a light, simple soup that makes a good beginning for a dinner with either version. Bread, salad, and fruit then round out the meal.

Serve a cold rosé or white wine from a jug, or beer—or cider, as they do in Brittany.

Spinach and Mushrooms

1½ pounds fresh spinach, or
    2 packages (10 ounces each)
      frozen chopped spinach
2 tablespoons butter
8 scallions, chopped

¾ pound mushrooms, coarsely
    chopped
⅛ teaspoon allspice
salt and pepper

Wash, trim off heavy stems, drain, and chop fresh spinach; or thaw, squeeze, and drain frozen spinach. In a heavy pot large enough to hold the fresh spinach, if that is what you are using, heat the butter and lightly sauté the scallions and mushrooms for about 1 minute, sprinkling with salt and pepper. Add the spinach and cook, stirring, until moisture has evaporated. Stir in pepper, allspice, and salt to taste. Set aside while you deal with Step 2.

Ham

1 tablespoon butter
1 pound cooked ham in ¼-inch
   dice

2 tablespoons Porto or Cream
   Sherry
1 teaspoon Dijon mustard
   pepper, and salt if needed

Heat the butter in a heavy skillet and cook the ham in it for about 1 minute. Pour in the Porto or Sherry and cook until it has almost evaporated. Stir in mustard. Salt and pepper to taste. Combine ham with spinach mixture.

Assembly and Finish

   Mornay sauce (recipe follows)
16 crêpes

¼ cup finely chopped parsley

Stir 2 tablespoons of Mornay sauce into the mixture to act as a kind of binder. The rest of the sauce will cover the filled crêpes for baking.

Butter a large, shallow baking dish or 2 smaller ones that will take the crêpes close together, side by side, in one layer. Spread a thin layer of Mornay sauce on the bottom of the dish or dishes.

Spread out 8 of the crêpes on waxed paper. Divide half the filling mixture among them, piling it down the middle of each crêpe, and folding the sides over. Place the crêpes in the baking dish, folded side down, and repeat with the rest.

Pour Mornay sauce over the middle of the crêpes, leaving about an inch of the crêpes bare on each side. Put a dab of butter on these exposed ends. Place uncovered in a preheated 350°F oven for 20 minutes, or until hot, bubbling, and spotted with golden brown here and there. Serve sprinkled with parsley.

Mornay Sauce

4 tablespoons butter
4 tablespoons flour
3 cups milk
½ teaspoon salt

¼ teaspoon white pepper
½ cup Jarlsberg cheese, coarsely
   grated

In a saucepan, melt the butter and stir in the flour. Off the heat, beat in the milk to make a smooth mixture. Back on the heat, add the salt and pepper, and cook, stirring constantly, until sauce thickens—2–3 minutes. Add cheese and stir until smooth.

Chicken and Spinach Crêpes

For a version of the ham and spinach crêpes using chicken instead, only Step 2 changes.

Use 2 whole boneless, skinless chicken breasts (about 1 pound), cut into ¾-inch to 1-inch pieces. Cook them in 2 tablespoons butter for about 4 minutes, until they are a little brown in places, turning constantly. Sprinkle with salt and pepper, add 2 tablespoons Amontillado Sherry, and, stirring to incorporate bits on the bottom of the pan, add to the spinach mixture. Omit the mustard in this version.

Stracciatelli

8 cups beef or chicken broth
½ cup grated Parmesan cheese

4 eggs, lightly beaten
freshly ground black pepper

Bring broth to a rolling boil. Mix cheese and eggs, and pour mixture slowly into broth. Simmer 2–3 minutes, stirring gently to keep particles small and separate. Add pepper and serve at once.

Ham and Mushroom Crêpes   *8 servings of 2 crêpes each*

A good beginning for a dinner with these crêpes is an easy and delightful broccoli soup (recipe given). Salad, bread, and fruit then complete the meal.

Serve a cold white jug wine with this, adjusted to taste with a squeeze of lemon, ice, and soda water.

16 crêpes

Filling

3 tablespoons butter
¼ cup minced scallions
1 pound sliced cooked ham,
    julienned
¾ pound mushrooms, minced
¼ cup sour cream
12 ounces cream cheese at room
    temperature

¼ cup minced fresh dill or
    1½ teaspoons dried dill
¼ cup freshly grated Parmesan
    cheese
salt and pepper to taste

Heat butter in a heavy skillet and put in scallions, ham, and mushrooms. Cook mixture over fairly high heat until moisture has evaporated.

Mix sour cream, cream cheese, dill, and Parmesan together. Taste and add salt and pepper to taste. Combine with ham mixture and check seasoning again. Chill for about 30 minutes before filling crêpes.

Tomato Sauce

1 garlic clove, minced
2 tablespoons olive oil

1 can (1 pound) tomatoes,
    crushed or chopped
salt and pepper

Cook garlic in oil a minute or two until soft. Add tomatoes and salt and pepper to taste. Cook 15 minutes.

Spread out the 16 crêpes on waxed paper or plastic wrap. Divide filling mixture among them, piling it down the middle of each crêpe, and folding the sides over.

Spread a thin layer of tomato sauce on the bottom of a large baking dish or 2 smaller ones that will take the crêpes close together, side by side, in one layer. Place the filled crêpes in the dish or dishes, folded side down. Pour tomato sauce down the middle of the crêpes, leaving about an inch of the crêpes bare on each side. Put a dab of butter on these exposed ends. Place uncovered in a preheated 350°F oven for 15–20 minutes, until heated through.

Broccoli Soup

1 bunch broccoli
3 cups water

6 chicken bouillon cubes
2 cups (1 pint) sour cream

Chop broccoli in small pieces, including well-peeled stems. Place bouillon cubes in water, bring to boil, add broccoli. Cook about 10 minutes, until just soft. Remove from heat. Purée, putting broccoli through food mill or food processor in batches. Stir in sour cream. Cool and chill.

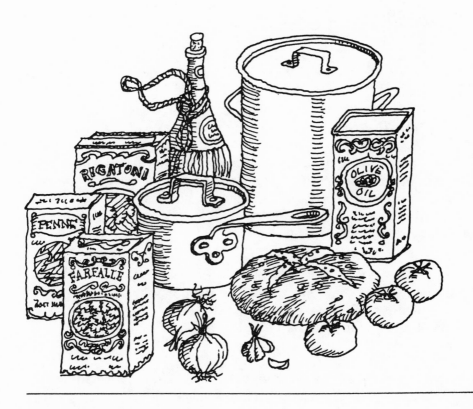

6. Pasta...
It Isn't All Spaghetti

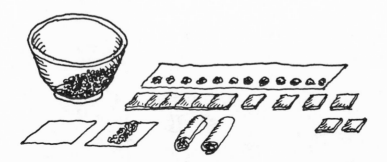

Your Own Pasta

The food processor and hand pasta machine take all the effort out of pasta making, besides cutting down on the time it takes. Homemade pasta cooks in a very short time, 2–3 minutes, and remember to reserve at least a cup of the cooking water in case it is too dry. It does soak up sauce voraciously; provide plenty.

Pasta   *makes 1 pound, 6–8 servings of noodles*

2 cups flour   1 teaspoon salt
3 jumbo eggs, or 3 large eggs
    plus 1 tablespoon oil, water
    if needed

If jumbo eggs are used: put flour, eggs, and salt in food processor with the steel blade, and process until dough forms a ball.

If large eggs are used: Put flour, eggs, oil, and salt into processor. If mixture is too dry to form a ball, add a teaspoon of water.

When ball forms, stop machine and let the dough rest for 2 minutes. Turn on the machine again and let the ball bump around for 10 seconds. This is the equivalent of kneading.

Take out the ball and wrap it in a clean cloth. Let it rest for 15 minutes. Then, on a floured board, flatten the ball to a rectangle 2″ thick. Cut into 4 pieces and lightly flour cut sides and top of dough.

Feed one of the quarters into the part of the pasta machine that looks like a wringer (the 2 parallel cylinders), setting the dial at the widest opening.* Turn the dial to the next widest opening and put the pasta through again. Repeat through the fifth opening for cannelloni or ravioli, through the sixth for noodles. If sheets of pasta get too long to manage, cut them into shorter lengths. Lay the sheets out on a clean cloth and go through the same procedure with the other 3 pieces of dough. Cut into appropriate shapes for cannelloni or ravioli. For noodles, feed the sheets into the cutter that makes the width you want.

Manicotti and Cannelloni

6 servings of 2 manicotti each
6 servings of 3 cannelloni each

Manicotti, meaning muff or sleeve, is the ribbed tube with diagonally cut ends, found in packages everywhere, and meant to be filled. Cannelloni, described in the dictionary as large macaroni, is fresh pasta in squares or rectangles, wrapped around a filling. Both are cooked before filling, covered with two sauces, and brought to bubbling hotness in the oven. Recipes for filling and sauces follow.

The dish is splendid enough to warrant a first course of oysters or clams on the half shell, or smoked salmon with capers, served with white wine like Frascati or Verdicchio. The pasta itself calls for a red wine—a Valpolicella, or a California Zinfandel or Gamay. A salad with lettuce and plenty of crisp vegetables might accompany it, followed by an extravagant pastry for dessert. Grappa and espresso could end the meal with an Italian flourish.

When starting the pasta through rollers, if dough is too sticky, take out and flour lightly, then put through again. Do the same if the sheet breaks apart. If the strands do not separate properly when passing through the cutter, set aside the sheets to dry for 5 minutes or so.

Filling

1 tablespoon oil
1 pound lean ground beef
1 package (10 ounces) frozen
    chopped spinach, or 1 pound
    fresh—cooked, drained,
    pressed dry, and finely
    chopped
½ cup freshly grated Parmesan
    cheese

¼ cup fine, dry bread crumbs
1 garlic clove, chopped
½ teaspoon salt, more if needed
¼ teaspoon pepper
½ teaspoon oregano
    dash of nutmeg
2 eggs, lightly beaten

Heat the oil in a skillet and crumble in the beef. Cook, stirring and breaking up lumps, until it is lightly brown. Pour off any fat. In a mixing bowl, combine the meat, spinach, Parmesan, and crumbs.

Mash the garlic with the salt until there are no large pieces, and add with the other seasonings to the eggs. Combine thoroughly with the meat mixture.

Butter a large, shallow baking dish or 2 smaller ones that will take the tubes or rolls close together, side by side, in one layer.

Cream Sauce

4 tablespoons butter
4 tablespoons flour
3 cups milk, warmed

¾ teaspoon salt, or to taste
¼ teaspoon white pepper

In a saucepan, melt the butter and stir in the flour. Take it off the heat and pour in the milk, stirring constantly until sauce is smooth. Put back on the heat and cook, stirring, until it comes to a boil. Add salt and pepper and cook 2–3 minutes, still stirring, until sauce thickens.

Tomato Sauce

1 tablespoon oil
1 small onion, finely chopped
    (about ½ cup)
1 garlic clove, minced
1 can (1 pound) Italian tomatoes,
    crushed or chopped

½ teaspoon oregano
1 small bay leaf
¼ cup freshly grated Parmesan
    cheese

Heat the oil in a saucepan and cook the onion and garlic in it until onion is soft but not brown. Add the tomatoes, oregano, and bay leaf. Cook 30–45 minutes, or until sauce is no longer watery.

The cheese is to sprinkle on top when the dish goes in the oven.

Manicotti
Drop manicotti tubes carefully into 6 quarts boiling water with 2 table spoons salt. Stir gently and cook 6 minutes after water comes back to a boil. Drain, rinse with cold water, and set on paper towels to drain some more. Using a butter knife or small spoon, put the filling into the tubes, and place them in the baking dish as they are filled.

Cannelloni
After putting pasta dough through opening 5 on the machine, you will have long strips 4 inches wide. Cut off 16 pieces 4 inches long, making 16 4-by-4-inch squares. This is about half of the pasta recipe. Cut the rest into squares and pile up with waxed paper between squares. Wrap well with plastic and freeze for another time.

Set salted water to boil in a large skillet or wide, shallow saucepan. Place 2 or 3 pasta squares at a time in the boiling water and cook just until they come to the top—2 or 3 minutes. Take the squares, now about 5 inches square, from the water and lay them on a clean cloth. Put about 2 table-spoons of filling down the middle, and roll them up, with the help of the cloth. Place, folded side down, in the baking dish.

If cream sauce has cooled and thickened, warm it up and stir smooth again. Pour over the tubes or rolls in the baking dish, to cover completely. Let stand for a few minutes to set. Spoon the tomato sauce over all, and sprinkle with Parmesan cheese.

Manicotti: Bake uncovered, in preheated 350°F oven for about 20 minutes—until hot, tender, and bubbling.

Cannelloni: Bake uncovered for about 15 minutes.

Ravioli

6 servings

These little pillows of filled pasta are so good when they are made with your own pasta that it is worth the effort. Since the ravioli, if not cooked the same day they are made, should be frozen, it might be well to make them ahead and cook them later, when the effort is long forgotten.

Use the filling given for cannelloni or manicotti, but use 2 egg yolks instead of 2 whole eggs, to make the filling drier. Also, sprinkle cornmeal on the plastic they will lie on when finished.

Make 3-inch strips of pasta dough through the fifth turn of the roller dial on the pasta machine. Cut off in 12-inch lengths for easier handling. Lay out the strips on table or counter.

With the short ends toward you, place little mounds of filling (a teaspoon or so), one finger apart, all the way up (or down) the right half of each strip until filling is used up. With a forefinger dipped in water, draw lines between the fillings and across the unfilled side of the strips. Do the same with the edges. This moistening will help the dough stick together.

Bring the left half of the strip over the filled side, and press down between the fillings and along the top, bottom, and side of the strip. Leave the left side unpressed, giving the fillings a little extra room.

Cut mounds apart with a sharp knife or pastry cutter, and place on plastic sheets that have been sprinkled with cornmeal. Allow ravioli to dry for 10–15 minutes. If they are to be used the same day, refrigerate in single layers, wrapped in plastic. For later use, freeze in single layers; when they are frozen, bag them.

Cook in boiling salted water or broth for 5–6 minutes, or until there is no floury taste. Serve with tomato sauce, or just butter and Parmesan cheese.

Farfalle con Salsiccie   *6 servings*

Farfalle means butterflies, and that is what these look like—unless you think they look like bow ties. Either way, they make a fine vehicle for a sauce of Italian sausages—sweet, hot, or half and half.

A big leafy salad, including some spinach; Italian bread and cheeses; and a dessert of fresh pineapple with a sprinkle of Kirsch could complete the meal.

White wines like Soave or Verdicchio go with the pasta, and a red like a California Petite Sirah goes with the cheese.

Sauce can be made ahead, or while water heats for the pasta.

Sauce
1 tablespoon dry or sweet Vermouth, or Marsala
1 pound Italian sausages, sweet and/or hot, removed from casings
1 tablespoon olive oil

1 small onion, chopped (½ cup)
1 garlic clove, minced
1 cup dry white wine
1 can (1 pound) Italian tomatoes, chopped
salt to taste

Put the Vermouth or Marsala in a large skillet and crumble in sausage meat. Cook until lightly browned, breaking up with a fork into more or less uniform chunks as it cooks. Remove sausage with a slotted spoon and reserve. Pour off all but 1 tablespoon of fat from pan.

Add olive oil, onion, and garlic. Cook over low heat until onion is limp and transparent. Add white wine and simmer until it has been reduced by half. Stir in tomatoes and sausage. Simmer partially covered for 15–20 minutes, until sauce is not watery. Taste and add salt if needed.

Pasta
1 pound farfalle
1 tablespoon olive oil
¼ cup finely chopped parsley

¼ cup freshly grated Romano or Parmesan cheese

Cook farfalle according to package directions, but do not overcook. Turn into large bowl with the oil. Add sauce and toss until thoroughly mixed. Stir in parsley and cheese. Serve promptly.

Rigatoni With Bolognese Sauce   *6–8 servings*

Rigatoni is large, ribbed macaroni. Of course spaghetti, thin noodles, or smaller, shaped pasta may be used with this sauce, but the taste will be different. The Bolognese is one of the few sauces that are rich and substantial enough for rigatoni, not only coating it, but finding its way into the tubes—and the tubes can stand up to the thorough mixing required. You will see when you try it why this combination of sauce and pasta is a natural.

Crisp vegetables with or without a dip would make an appropriately light first course; salad could be a simple one with mixed greens; and dessert, apples and Gorgonzola.

You could serve a good Italian wine with this—a Barolo or Gattinara—and end the meal in style with espresso and Strega.

4 tablespoons butter
2 slices bacon, diced
1 medium onion, finely chopped
1 medium carrot, finely chopped
1 celery stalk, finely chopped
1 pound lean ground beef
⅓ cup dry white wine
   salt, pepper, and oregano
2 cups canned Italian tomatoes
   in tomato paste
½–1 cup beef broth

2 whole chicken livers, chopped
¼ pound mushrooms, chopped
1 garlic clove, minced
½–1 cup heavy cream
¼ cup finely chopped parsley for
   garnish

1 pound rigatoni, cooked
   according to package
   directions

Heat 1 tablespoon of the butter in a large, deep skillet or sauté pan that has a lid. Cook bacon in butter until it is golden. Add onion, carrot, and celery, cover, and cook on low heat for a few minutes until onions are soft, stirring occasionally.

Crumble meat into vegetables and cook over fairly high heat, stirring and breaking up lumps, until meat is beginning to brown and mixture is almost dry. Moisten with wine and cook until wine evaporates. Season with salt, pepper, and oregano, and don't make it too bland (about ½ teaspoon oregano, about 1 teaspoon salt, and plenty of pepper).

Add tomatoes, breaking them up with your hand as you add them. Add ¼ cup broth, cover, and cook on low heat for 1 hour. Check during cooking. Sauce should lose any wateriness and get quite thick, thicker than the usual sauce because it is to have cream added to it. However, if it gets so thick there is danger of sticking along the way, add small amounts of broth If it is still watery after the hour, cook another 15 minutes.

In a small skillet, heat 1 tablespoon of the butter, and put in livers, mushrooms, and garlic. Cook until liquid evaporates, and add to sauce. Cook sauce another 10 minutes, then add cream to achieve desired thickness. Cook until hot again. Stir in remaining 2 tablespoons butter and check seasoning. Mix thoroughly with cooked, drained rigatoni, and sprinkle parsley on top.

Penne With Ham and Asparagus Sauce   *6 servings*

Penne are 1–1½-inch oval tubes with the ends cut at parallel diagonals. The word means feathers, and you can see that the ends look like the tips of quill pens. This sauce of ham, asparagus, cream, and Parmesan seems to suit the pasta.

A chilled white wine—Soave or Verdicchio, a salad of tomatoes and fresh basil, French or Italian bread, and fruit of the season is all you need for a fine spring dinner.

1 pound penne	½ cup freshly grated Parmesan
1 pound asparagus	cheese
2 tablespoons butter	salt and freshly ground black
1 pound sliced cooked ham in	pepper to taste
julienne strips	chopped parsley for garnish
1 cup heavy cream	

Set 6 quarts of water with 2 tablespoons of salt, to boil, for the pasta. In another large pot, heat salted water for the asparagus. Trim the stem ends of the asparagus, and peel the stems down to the palest green. Cut into 2-inch pieces. Cook the asparagus for 5 minutes, or a little more if the stalks are large, just until they are barely tender. Drain and run under cold water to prevent further cooking.

Heat butter in a large, heavy skillet or wide, shallow pan. Put in the asparagus and ham and cook, stirring, until they are hot. Stir in cream and ¼ cup of the Parmesan cheese. Cook until everything is hot and well mixed. Taste and add salt and pepper. Add the rest of the cheese, or serve it on the side.

When the pasta is cooked but still slightly firm, drain and toss with the sauce. Serve sprinkled with parsley.

7. Stuffed Vegetables...
Better Than You Think

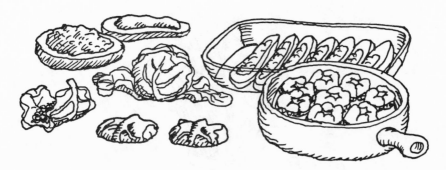

Stuffed Eggplant

6 servings

A leafy salad with cucumbers, and lemon in the dressing, crusty bread, cheese, and fruit are enough to make a fine meal with the eggplants. For the famished, a starchy accompaniment could be rice pilaf with almonds (recipe given), or homemade pasta served with just butter and Parmesan.

Light, young wines are best with this—everything from the dry tartness of a Muscadet of the Loire or the crisp floweriness of a Rhine or Moselle to the fruitiness of a California Chenin Blanc.

Eggplants

3 medium eggplants, about 1
    pound each, shiny, firm,
    unspotted, flat rather than
    dimpled on the bottom, long
    rather than squat

2 tablespoons olive oil
    salt and pepper

Wash eggplants and trim off stem ends. Slice in half lengthwise and scoop out pulp, leaving a shell ½ inch thick. Coarsely chop the pulp. Paint the shells with olive oil and sprinkle lightly with salt and pepper. Heat the rest of this batch of oil in a large, heavy, lidded skillet, and quickly sauté the pulp, tossing and adding more oil if necessary. Sprinkle with a little salt and pepper, remove from the skillet, and set aside.

146

Filling

1 tablespoon olive oil
1 medium onion, finely chopped
    (1 cup)
2 garlic cloves, minced
1 pound lean ground lamb
2 cups canned Italian tomatoes,
    chopped or mashed
1¼ teaspoons salt
½ teaspoon freshly ground black
    pepper

1 teaspoon oregano
½ teaspoon thyme
6 tablespoons finely chopped
    parsley (4 tablespoons
    reserved for garnish)
⅓ cup uncooked rice
2 tablespoons lemon juice
6 tablespoons Parmesan cheese
    for topping

Wipe the skillet to remove bits of eggplant. Put in olive oil, onions, and garlic, and cook until onions are soft but not brown. Crumble in lamb and cook, stirring and breaking up lumps, until meat has lost its pink color and has dried a bit but is not quite brown. Turn off heat, tip the pan, push meat back from the edge, and spoon out and discard any fat that has gathered

With skillet back on the heat, add tomatoes, seasonings, 2 tablespoons of the parsley, and rice. Bring to a simmer, cover, and cook on very low flame for 20 minutes.

Remove from heat and stir in lemon juice and eggplant pulp. Fill the shells with mixture and place side by side in oiled baking dish or casserole, close together. Use 2 dishes if necessary. Sprinkle each with about 1 tablespoon Parmesan. Cover with lid or foil and bake in preheated 325°F oven for 40 minutes, or until shells are tender but still hold their shape. Fluff the filling gently with a fork before sprinkling with parsley.

Rice Pilaf With Almonds

2 tablespoons butter
1½ cups rice
1 medium onion, finely chopped
    (1 cup)
3 cups canned chicken broth,
    fat removed from top
1 teaspoon turmeric

salt and pepper
2 tablespoons butter
⅓ cup slivered almonds
⅓ cup raisins (optional) soaked
    in boiling water for 10
    minutes

Melt butter in a heavy, lidded saucepan or casserole. Put in rice and onion and cook slowly until onion is transparent and rice opaque. Remove from heat.

In another saucepan, heat broth to boiling, with turmeric, and add to rice mixture in first pan. Back on the heat, stir once and bring to a boil. Turn heat down, cover, and cook on low heat for 20–25 minutes, or until rice is cooked and liquid absorbed. Fluff with a fork and check seasoning, adding salt and pepper if needed.

Toast almonds in a small amount of butter, and stir into rice with the rest of the butter and the drained raisins, if used.

Spanish-American Cabbage Rolls   *6 servings of 2 rolls each*

Rice and beans, served separately or mixed together, would be likely accompaniments to these stuffed cabbage leaves. Or the beans could be served in salad form—red kidney beans in oil and vinegar, with plenty of chopped scallions. The rolls taste good served with sour cream, especially if you increase the amount of green chilies called for in the recipe. Crusty bread and a dessert of assorted melon wedges or a custard could round out the meal.

A hearty red jug wine from Spain, Portugal, Italy, or California, or beer, would be suitable to drink with the rolls.

The cabbage rolls are even better re-heated the following day.

1 medium-size green cabbage
2 slices stale homemade-style
    bread, crusts removed
⅓ cup water
1 pound ground beef
1 small onion, finely chopped
    (½ cup)
1 clove garlic, minced
¼ cup canned green chilies,
    chopped (not jalapeños)
1 egg, lightly beaten

1½ teaspoons salt
1 teaspoon cumin
½ cup coarsely grated sharp
    Cheddar cheese (2 ounces)

1 can (2 pounds, 3 ounces)
    Italian tomatoes, chopped
1 medium green pepper, seeded,
    deribbed, chopped
1 teaspoon salt, or to taste

Trim off any bad leaves from cabbage and cut out about 3 inches of core. Immerse in boiling water. As soon as outer leaves are slightly limp and can be removed, take them off with tongs and set to drain. Keep water boiling and remove leaves as they will come until you have 12 good ones. When leaves get small, you may need 2 to equal 1 larger one. See Note.

Tear bread into coarse crumbs and soak in the water for 2–3 minutes. Add, with any unabsorbed water, to meat in a mixing bowl, along with onions, garlic, and chilies. Mix egg with salt and cumin, and combine with meat mixture. Stir in cheese and mix thoroughly.

Place a mound of filling on each cabbage leaf, fold the sides of the leaf over filling, and roll up from root end to tip. Secure with toothpicks, and set in one layer in a baking dish or large, shallow casserole. Mix sauce ingredients together and pour over rolls. Cover with foil or lid and place in preheated 350°F oven for 1 hour. If sauce has cooked down too much, add a little water.

For later serving: cool, loosely covered, to room temperature. Cover and refrigerate. Reheat in preheated 350°F oven, covered, for 25 to 30 minutes, or until heated through.

Note: If you do not like to encounter the still-firm ribs of the cabbage leaves after they are cooked, cut them out before rolling.

Ham-Filled Zucchini

6 servings

Handsome to begin with, these zucchini boats look particularly beautiful on a platter with plenty of parsley or watercress among them. The filling is ham and tomatoes, with a creamy cheese sauce on top, lightly browned, and capers within.

Serve with rice or thin noodles, and for color and taste, buttered carrots, cut on a sharp diagonal. Crusty bread, salad, and dessert from a fine pastry shop could make a meal to be proud of.

White wine goes with the zucchini—a Muscadet or an Italian Frascati, if you can find it.

Once baked, the filled zucchini do not freeze or reheat well.

Mornay Sauce
2 tablespoons butter
3 tablespoons flour
1½ cups milk
1½ teaspoons Dijon mustard

½ cup coarsely grated sharp
    Cheddar cheese
salt and pepper

In a saucepan, melt butter and stir in flour to make a smooth paste. Off the heat, stir in milk until smooth. Back on heat, cook, stirring constantly, until mixture boils and thickens. Add mustard, cheese, and salt and pepper to taste. Set aside to cool, stirring occasionally to prevent skin from forming.

Zucchini
4 zucchini, ¾–1 pound each,
    firm, unblemished, not too
    long and narrow

Wash zucchini and trim off ends. Do not peel. Blanch zucchini in boiling salted water for 5 minutes. Drain and run cold water over them to prevent further cooking.

Halve zucchini lengthwise and scoop out pulp, leaving a ½-inch shell. Set shells, skin side down, and pulp to drain on paper towels.

Filling
2 tablespoons butter
¼ cup finely chopped scallions
    or shallots
1 garlic clove, minced
4 medium tomatoes, peeled,
    seeded, chopped, or 1 cup
    canned tomatoes, drained
    and chopped

1 tablespoon capers, drained
    (more if desired)
1 pound cooked ham, in ½-inch
    dice

Melt butter in a saucepan and cook scallions or shallots and garlic until soft but not brown. Add zucchini pulp and tomatoes and cook over fairly high heat until hot and almost dry. Sprinkle with salt and pepper. Stir in capers, ham, and ¼ cup of the Mornay sauce.

Assembly and Finish

4 tablespoons freshly grated
    Parmesan cheese for tops

¼ cup finely chopped parsley for
    garnish

Sprinkle shells with salt and pepper, and fill with ham mixture. Spoon Mornay sauce over each filled shell and sprinkle with Parmesan.

Set filled shells in oiled baking dish or dishes, and bake, uncovered, in preheated 425° F oven for 10 minutes, or until lightly browned. Serve sprinkled with parsley.

Sausage-Stuffed Green Peppers
6 servings

Apples, walnuts, and rye bread crumbs are mixed with the sausage meat to make these unusual stuffed peppers. The peppers are not cooked until they are soft, either, which may come as a surprise, and they are cooked in chicken broth rather than the customary tomatoes. A suggestion for a sauce made with the chicken broth is given at the end of the recipe.

Serve with mashed potatoes and a buttered vegetable of the season. Salad and a cheese tray could follow, and dessert could be rich, since the peppers do not make a heavy main course.

A German wine marked Kabinett, from the Rhine, would be good with the peppers because of the slight sweetness of the apples in the filling.

6 medium green peppers—
    choose ones that will
    stand alone
1 small onion, finely chopped
    (½ cup)
1 pound bulk sausage meat
2 garlic cloves, whole
2–4 slices firm, stale caraway rye
    bread, torn into crumbs to
    make 2 cups
¼ teaspoon red-pepper flakes
    (or to taste)

⅛ teaspoon each sage, crumbled
    rosemary, and allspice
    salt to taste
⅓ cup chopped walnuts in
    ¼-inch pieces
1 firm green apple, peeled, cored,
    in ½-inch dice
1 egg, lightly beaten

1½–2 cups chicken broth
    pimientos and parsley for
    garnish

Wash peppers and cut off tops at a point where the tops can be kept intact with stem, and used as lids. Remove seeds and ribs from inside peppers, and sprinkle with salt. Rub a little oil on tops. Set tops and bottoms aside.

In a lidded, heavy skillet, casserole, or wide, shallow saucepan, cook onions and sausage without adding fat until sausage loses its pink color. Stir and break up lumps with a fork as sausage cooks. Bury garlic cloves in the mixture. Cover and cook on very low heat for 15 minutes. Remove from heat, fish out garlic and discard, and pour off fat.

Stir in bread crumbs and seasonings. Taste and add salt if needed (sausages vary in saltiness). Stir in apple, walnuts, and egg. Fill peppers lightly with mixture, mounding it on top. Put lids on without pressing down filling, and affix lids with toothpicks, leaving space between top and bottom. Set peppers in a baking dish, and pour in chicken broth to the depth of about ¾ inch on the bottom, reserving any broth left over. Bake in preheated 350°F oven, uncovered, for 20 minutes, or until peppers are just tender but not mushy or collapsing.

Serve on a warm platter, lavishly embellished with parsley sprigs, and with coarsely chopped pimientos strewn over all.

To make a sauce: Pour cooking broth into a two-cup measuring cup. Add any reserved broth or water to make 1½ cups. Mix together 2 tablespoons flour and 2 tablespoons soft butter. In a small saucepan, bring broth to a boil and stir in flour-butter mixture. Cook until thick. Check seasoning and add salt and pepper to taste.

8. Main-Course Soups and Salads... for a Change of Pace

MAIN-COURSE SOUPS

Having soup as a main course allows one to enjoy it to the fullest, no matter how rich and substantial it is, because there is no main course coming to save room for. The salad that follows can be a fancy one, with all kinds of things in it, including fruit and nuts. Assorted breads and cheeses and a sumptuous dessert complete the meal.

To make an occasion of this kind of meal, present the soup in a tureen, enameled ironware pot, Dutch oven, or even the big stockpot it was cooked in. The meal can be sit-down style or buffet. For a buffet, soup is easier to handle in large mugs. At the table, you can get out the best china if you like. If the bowls are small, intended for a dainty serving or consommé, they can be filled again.

Main-course soups are great to take to ski lodge or summer cottage. Made ahead, cooled, and refrigerated, the soup can be taken along in its cooking pot, ready to be put on the fire while the car is being unpacked.

Beef and Bean Soup with Pistou Sauce   8–10 *servings*

A rich, substantial soup, this needs only crusty bread and a salad of assorted greens to make a meal. To make it go further, or for hearty appetites, it could be preceded by seafood and followed by a cheese tray and fruit.

One of the inexpensive Italian red wines is good with the soup.

1 pound dried beans—Great
   Northern, navy, or baby limas
10 cups water
1 pound stewing beef, in ¾-inch
   to 1-inch pieces
2 medium onions, chopped
2 carrots, chopped
2 stalks celery, chopped

1 can (1 pound) tomatoes,
   mashed or chopped
½ teaspoon oregano
1 tablespoon salt
   pepper to taste
¼ cup olive oil
2 tablespoons vinegar

Put beans in a large pot with 10 cups of water. Bring to a boil, turn off heat, and allow to stand for 1 hour. Add meat and bring to a boil again. Maintain a gentle boil, and skim off foam as it appears. When no more foam is appearing, turn down to a simmer and add onions, garlic, carrots, celery, and tomatoes. Simmer for 30 minutes. Add oregano, salt, pepper to taste, and olive oil. Cook 30 minutes longer. Check and add salt if needed; add vinegar and simmer another 10 minutes, or until beans and meat are tender.

Pistou Sauce

4 garlic cloves, chopped
¼ cup chopped fresh basil leaves
   (or if you must, 1½ tablespoons dried basil)

⅓ cup freshly grated Parmesan
   cheese
¼ cup tomato paste
¼–½ cup olive oil

Pistou Sauce: Put garlic, basil, Parmesan, and tomato paste into blender. Start blender, pour in oil very slowly, and blend until sauce has the consistency of mayonnaise. Stir into the soup.

Pistou can be served separately, so diners can add as much or as little as they want.

Beef and Beet Soup   *8–10 servings (about 3½ quarts)*

This is not a heavy soup, but it is satisfying because of the potatoes in it. Serve with sour cream and black bread.

1 pound boneless stewing beef, in ¾-inch pieces
6 cups water (all or part of this can be beef broth, and less salt will be needed)
2 medium onions, finely chopped
1 cup tomato purée
  liquid from 4 1-pound cans beets (reserve beets)

1 tablespoon salt
¼ teaspoon pepper
  juice of 1 lemon
1 tablespoon cider vinegar
2 tablespoons brown sugar
8 medium potatoes (not baking potatoes), boiled, peeled, in ¾-inch dice
  parsley for garnish

Put the beef into a large (6-quart) stock or spaghetti pot. Pour in the water and bring to a boil. Boil gently for a few minutes, skimming off foam as it appears. When foam stops forming, add everything else except potatoes, parsley, and the beets. Bring to a boil, turn down to a simmer, and simmer partially covered for 30 minutes. Purée the beets and add them. Continue to simmer for another 20 minutes, or until beef is tender. Add potatoes and cook until potatoes are hot. Taste and add salt if needed—potatoes absorb salt.

Lentil and Sausage Soup   *8–10 servings (about 2½ quarts)*

This is a substantial soup, good with rye bread.

1 slice bacon, diced
3 garlic cloves, minced
2 medium onions, finely chopped (2 cups)
2 stalks celery, finely chopped (1 cup)
2 tablespoons finely chopped parsley

¼ cup dry red wine
1 pound lentils
4 cups water
6 cups beef broth
2 teaspoons salt
½ teaspoon pepper
1 teaspoon oregano
1 bay leaf

1 pound Polish sausage, knackwurst, or other smoked, cooked sausage, in slices, skinned if necessary, and lightly sautéed in 1 tablespoon butter

In a large, lidded stockpot or Dutch oven, cook the bacon on low heat, separating the morsels as they cook. Cook until golden brown. Stir in garlic, onion, and celery and parsley. Cover and cook, still on low heat, until vegetables are beginning to soften, but not brown.

Pour in wine and cook until wine has almost evaporated. Wash and pick over lentils, discarding any foreign matter or shriveled beans. Add to vegetables with water, broth, salt, pepper, oregano, and bay leaf. Cover and simmer 30 minutes, or until lentils are tender. (As with all beans, times can vary—keep checking).

When beans are tender, soup can be puréed—all of it or just part, 2 cups at a time. I like to purée about one third and leave the rest of the beans and vegetables visible.

Cook the sausage slices briefly in butter and add to the soup.

MAIN-COURSE SALADS

Putting a little meat in a salad does not turn the salad into a roast-beef dinner, but it does make it more satisfying, and worthy of being the focus of a fine meal. Besides, a salad meal is fun.

What to have with the salad is the question. There is bread—a basket of different kinds, a tray of cheeses, cold seafood or poached fish with mayonnaise, hard-boiled eggs (if there are none in the salad), pickles, relishes, and nuts, to name a few choices. As for dessert, this might be the kind of meal on which to splurge and serve several.

Young, fresh wines are best with salads, traditional choices being rosés, or reds like Beaujolais. Light, dry white wines—from the Loire, the Rhine, or the Italian north—enhance most salads, as do California bottlings like Sauvignon Blanc, Chenin Blanc, and Colombard. Great wines call for subtly flavored foods; there is little point in wasting their wonders on hearty salads (Champagne and sparkling wines may be an exception). Simple wines are best with salads, and while jug wines are generally bland, they can be made more sprightly with a squeeze of lemon, a splash of soda water, and some ice.

Chicken or Turkey Salad Savoyarde   *6 servings*

Curry in the dressing makes this salad unusual, as do its main ingredients—endive, apple, and cheese. Walnuts and black olives add texture and taste, and the chicken or turkey make it substantial enough for a main course.

Dressing

2 tablespoons wine or cider vinegar
1 teaspoon Dijon mustard
¼ teaspoon salt

⅛ teaspoon pepper
1½ teaspoons curry powder
6 tablespoons salad oil

Blend all ingredients except oil. Beat in oil.

Salad

1 pound (about 2½ cups) cooked chicken or turkey, in ½-inch dice
2 large endive in ½-inch rounds
1 large apple, peeled, cored, in ½-inch dice

6 ounces Gruyère, Jarlsberg, or Swiss cheese, in ½-inch dice
⅓ cup chopped walnuts
10–12 pitted black olives
Boston lettuce

Up to 30 minutes before serving, combine all salad ingredients except lettuce in a mixing bowl, and pour dressing over. Toss gently, and toss again once or twice before serving. Line a salad bowl with lettuce and put the salad with dressing in the middle. Serve some lettuce with each portion of salad.

Vinaigrette or French Dressing   *makes 1 cup*

This is a dressing for the salads which follow.

¼ cup wine vinegar
1 teaspoon Dijon mustard, or ¼ teaspoon dry mustard
½ teaspoon salt

¼ teaspoon freshly ground black pepper
¾ cup olive oil, salad oil, or a combination

Mix together everything but the oil. Beat in the oil. Taste and adjust seasoning.

Mediterranean Salad With Rice
8–10 servings

1 pound cooked ham, in ½-inch cubes

3 medium tomatoes, peeled, seeded, and chopped

1 medium green pepper, in thin strips

1 small red onion, finely chopped

1 can (2 ounces) anchovies, drained and chopped

2 tablespoons capers, drained

10 pitted black olives—5 chopped, 5 whole

10 pitted green olives—5 chopped, 5 whole

1 cup vinaigrette

3 cups cold cooked rice

3 hard-boiled eggs, quartered

¼ cup finely chopped parsley

Mix everything except rice, eggs, parsley, and whole olives with ½ cup vinaigrette. Stir in rice; add more dressing to taste. Arrange whole olives and eggs on top, and sprinkle with parsley.

Ham and Cheese Salade Niçoise
8–10 servings

4 ripe tomatoes, in wedges

2 cups cold cooked grean beans, in 2-inch pieces

2 cups cold cooked potatoes, in ¾-inch cubes

1 large head Boston lettuce or 1 small Boston and 1 romaine, washed, separated, and dried

1 pound sliced cooked ham, in julienne strips

1 pound Swiss or Jarlsberg cheese, in julienne strips

1 cucumber, peeled, seeded, in ¾-inch dice

1 bunch scallions, chopped, including green tops

3 hard-boiled eggs, quartered

½ cup pitted black olives

1 cup vinaigrette dressing

A few minutes before serving, put tomatoes, beans, and potatoes into the bottom of a salad bowl, and moisten with small amount of vinaigrette. Line bowl with greens and put in everything else, with eggs and olives on top. At serving time, pour vinaigrette over all and toss.

Bean and Sausage Salad

8–10 servings

1 pound dried white beans
   (Great Northern, navy, or
   baby lima beans), cooked
2 medium cucumbers, peeled,
   seeded, in ¾-inch dice
2 medium tomatoes, coarsely
   chopped
2 small (2½-inch diameter) red
   onions in thin slices,
   separated into rings

1 large green pepper, seeded,
   deribbed, in ¼-inch dice
4 whole pimientos, coarsely
   chopped
1 pound Polish sausage (kielbasa)
   in ¼-inch slices
1 cup vinaigrette dressing
   salad greens

Put dressing on salad ingredients up to an hour before serving. Start with ½ cup; add as much more as needed. Serve on lettuce leaves.

To cook dried beans: Wash and pick over beans, removing foreign matter like stones, and shriveled beans. Cover with 8 cups water and bring to a boil. Remove from heat and soak for 1 hour. Bring to a simmer, and simmer partially covered for 45 minutes to 1 hour or more. Add 2 teaspoons salt after 30 minutes of cooking. The timing is infuriatingly hard to predict—keep checking. Beans are done when they are tender but not mushy, and the skin lifts and flutters when you blow on them. When they are done, drain—and save the cooking water; it makes a fine soup base.

Chicken, Rice, and Bean Salad

8 servings

1 pound (about 2½ cups) cooked
   chicken or turkey, in 1–1½-
   inch pieces
3 cups cold cooked rice
2 cans (1 pound each) red
   kidney beans, drained and
   rinsed
2 medium tomatoes, in 1-inch
   pieces

1 large red onion, finely
   chopped (1½ cups)
1 large cucumber, peeled, halved,
   seeded, cut into ½-inch cubes
¼ cup finely chopped parsley
1 cup vinaigrette dressing, plus
   2 tablespoons additional
   vinegar
   lettuce (optional)

Mix all ingredients except lettuce and toss carefully with dressing. Taste and add salt and pepper if needed. Chill for an hour before serving, if possible, stirring occasionally. If lettuce is used, tuck in around the edge of the bowl and serve along with, not mixed into, the salad.

Beef Salad

6–8 servings

1 pound (about 2½ cups) cooked
    beef, preferably boiled, in
    small pieces
3 cups cold cooked rice
3 medium green peppers,
    seeded, deribbed, cut in strips
2 medium red onions, sliced in
    rounds (about 2 cups)
    pinch of saffron

¼ cup finely chopped parsley
½ cup vinaigrette dressing, more
    if needed
¼ cup pitted green olives
1 cantaloupe, seeded, peeled, in
    slices

Mix beef, rice, peppers, onions, saffron, and parsley with vinaigrette. Taste and add salt, pepper, and more dressing, if needed. Decorate with olives and melon slices.

9. Top-of-the-Stove Concoctions

Vegetables, Beans, and Sausages

6–8 servings

This used to be one of our campfire meals, without the nicety of pre-cooking the sausages and blotting them on paper towels. The vegetables were variable, according to what was to be found. It always seemed to taste good no matter what went into it. This version—enjoyed indoors, around a real table—was good too. For salad we had spinach, oranges, and scallions in an oil-and-vinegar dressing, and it was just right. Rioja wine, bread, and cheese completed the meal.

1 pound hot Italian sausages
    (or sweet, if you prefer)
2 tablespoons olive oil
3 small green peppers, in ¼-inch
    rings
3 medium red onions, in ¼-inch
    rings
3 garlic cloves, minced
1 medium zucchini, in ¼-inch
    slices

1 teaspoon salt
½ teaspoon pepper
½ teaspoon fennel seeds, crushed
1 teaspoon oregano
2 cans (1 pound each) black
    beans (or red kidney beans,
    or garbanzos), drained

Prick sausages and put them with ½ inch of water into a Dutch oven or large, deep skillet or flameproof casserole that will accommodate the vegetables before they subside with cooking. Cook sausages until water evaporates, and then until brown. Set them aside to drain on paper towels.

Pour off all but a film of fat from sausages, and put in olive oil. Put in everything else except beans and cook, stirring gently, until vegetables are tender but not too soft. Cut sausages into 1-inch pieces and stir carefully, with beans, into vegetables. Check seasoning and cook until heated through.

Stir-Fry Chicken

6–8 servings

Anyone familiar with genuine Chinese cooking can tell that this dish was devised a long way from China, but it tastes good and uses the wok in a way many Americans are doing these days. Instead of several small amounts of different things, a large wok is used to make one batch of some flavorful combination, mostly vegetables—and sometimes there is nothing Chinese about it. In this recipe the flavorings, though somewhat bizarre, are Chinese.

Thanks to some of our new Oriental citizens, who have opened attractive shops all over the country, supplies for their cuisine are now more widely available.

When I was served—and enjoyed—this dish, out in the boondocks of middle America, it was served with rice and a green salad, after a first course of a little homemade pasta with butter and Parmesan cheese. We drank Champagne with the meal, and had another bottle in lieu of dessert. It was wonderful.

1 pound boneless, skinless chicken breasts (2 small whole breasts), in ¾-inch to 1-inch pieces

Marinade
1 cup soy sauce
1 teaspoon hoisin sauce
1 teaspoon plum sauce
1 tablespoon honey
⅛ teaspoon (dash) hot oil (red oil, hot sauce, chili oil, or hot-pepper oil)

¼ cup Amontillado Sherry (medium dry)
1 teaspoon grated fresh ginger
1 tablespoon chopped scallions

Mix marinade ingredients together and add the chicken. Allow to stand for 1 hour, or as long as overnight.

Cook in large wok

2–3 tablespoons oil
  1 tablespoon finely chopped
    onion
  1 garlic clove, minced
    heavy stems from 1 bunch
      broccoli, trimmed, peeled
      down to palest green, in
      ⅛-inch slices
  1 medium sweet potato, peeled,
    quartered, in ⅛-inch slices

small, uniform flowerets from
  1 bunch broccoli
1 6–7-inch yellow summer
  squash, peeled, in ⅛-inch
  slices
¼ pound mushrooms, sliced
2 tablespoons chopped scallions

Heat oil in wok. Put in onions and garlic, and cook 30 seconds. Add chicken and marinade, and cook until chicken is firm to the touch, 1–2 minutes. Remove chicken from wok with slotted spoon and set aside.

Put broccoli stem slices into wok. Cook a minute or two. Put sweet potato slices in, cook a minute or two. Add broccoli flowerets, squash, mushrooms, and scallions, stirring and cooking briefly after each addition. Put the chicken back in to heat, and serve immediately, from the wok, with rice.

Hot Potato Salad and Sausage

6 servings

This version of a famous French first course makes it into a main course, hearty and satisfying because the flavors are strong. The sausages are hot Italian and the dressing is a nicely sharp vinaigrette. Scallions—the white part slightly cooked, the green added as a garnish—supply more flavor. The whole thing is done on top of the stove in a few minutes.

If you don't mind the butter needed for a hot vegetable (after all those potatoes), broccoli or carrots would be a good accompaniment. When tomatoes are really at their best, they can be served with nothing on them but salt, pepper, and fresh basil or finely chopped parsley. The rest of the year, a salad for this dinner can be made of firm tomatoes, avoiding oil and vinegar. Cut the tomatoes into chunks, stir with plenty of salt, pepper, finely chopped parsley, a little sugar and lemon juice. Add sugar and lemon juice in small amounts until the taste is right, and let the mixture stand for half an hour.

Beer is best for this meal.

Vinaigrette

3 tablespoons vinegar
½ teaspoon Dijon mustard
½ teaspoon salt
¼ teaspoon freshly ground black
    pepper

9 tablespoons salad oil, olive oil,
    or a combination

Mix all ingredients except oil. Beat in oil.

1 pound Italian hot sausages
    (or sweet, if you prefer)
3 bunches scallions, white part
    chopped, good green tops
    cut across in ¼-inch slices
    to make little circles

4 cups boiled potatoes (about
    1½ pounds), preferably new,
    peeled, in ¼-inch slices, at
    room temperature

Prick sausages and place in a 12-inch skillet, casserole, or sauté pan. (You need a wide pan so potatoes will heat quickly, without too much turning.) Put ½ inch of water in pan, and cook sausages until water evaporates. Lower heat and cook sausages until brown. Set aside on paper towels to drain.

Pour off all fat from pan, and pour in vinaigrette, stirring to incorporate morsels on bottom of pan. Add chopped white part of onions, bring to a boil, and put in potatoes. Turn down heat and cook, turning and stirring carefully to heat through. Slice sausages in 1-inch pieces and stir with potatoes to heat. When everything is hot, serve sprinkled with as much of the green scallion circles as needed.

Dilled Chicken and Potatoes

6–8 servings

Fresh dill is essential for this pleasantly satisfying, quickly made main dish. The chicken and potatoes are already cooked, and warm up with scallions, green peppers, and celery cooked in butter. Dill, capers, and plenty of salt and pepper are the seasonings, and the whole thing heats up finally in sour cream. Hard-boiled eggs are the garnish.

A green salad with tomatoes, or endive and beets would supply color, and dark bread would be better than white. Cheese and fruit make a good dessert—apples and Roquefort, pears and Brie, for instance.

To drink, try a Vinho Verde from Portugal, or Muscadet.

1 pound cooked chicken (or
   turkey), about 2½ cups
   in small pieces
3 tablespoons butter
3 bunches scallions, chopped
2 medium green peppers, finely
   chopped
1½ cups finely chopped celery
3 cups cooked potatoes,
   preferably new, in ¾-inch
   dice, at room temperature

3 tablespoons capers, drained,
   chopped if large
⅓ cup chopped fresh dill
1½ cups sour cream, mixed with
   5 teaspoons flour and ½ cup
   water

4 hard-boiled eggs, quartered
   sprigs of dill

Salt and pepper the chicken and set aside. (Salt and pepper is added to everything along the way in this dish, rather than all at once.) In a Dutch oven or the equivalent, melt butter, add scallions, green peppers, and celery. Cook until vegetables have softened slightly, sprinkling with salt and pepper. Carefully stir in potatoes, capers, and dill. Cook on low heat until hot, stirring from time to time. Taste and add salt and pepper as needed. Add chicken and sour-cream mixture, and cook until just bubbling. Serve on hot plates, garnished with eggs and dill sprigs.

Variation
This may be done with julienned ham, too. Omit the salt and pepper at the beginning, unless the ham is unusually bland. Add a couple of teaspoons of Dijon mustard to the sour-cream mixture.

INDEX

LIST OF SUPPLEMENTARY RECIPES